T HE second ^ MAGPIE CAFÉ COOK BOOK

By Ian Robson & Paul Gildroy

with a foreword by Brian Turner CBE

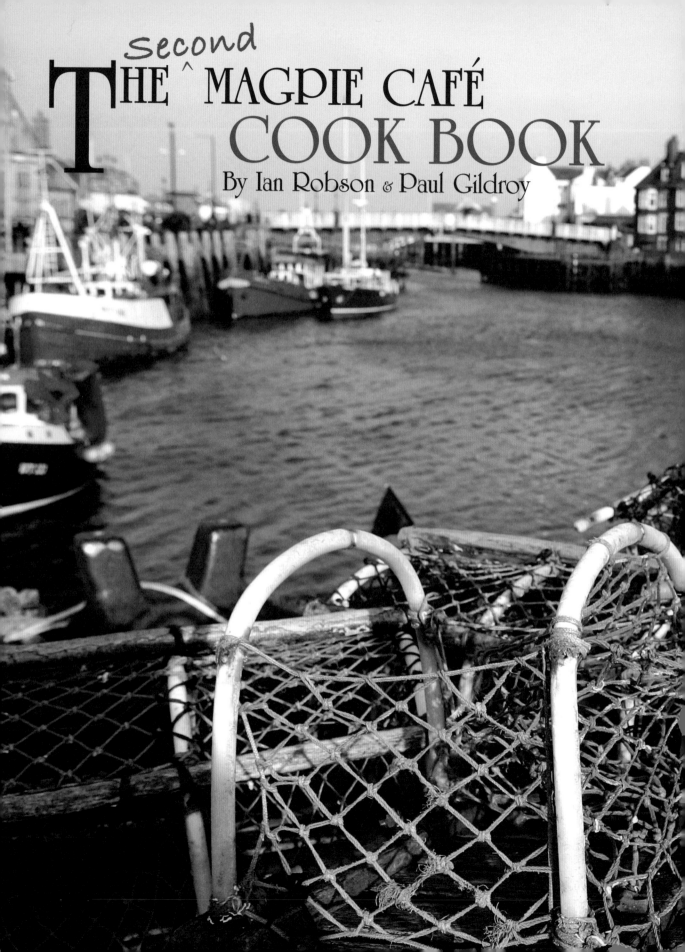

The second ^ MAGPIE CAFÉ COOK BOOK

By Ian Robson & Paul Gildroy

FOREWORD
BY BRIAN TURNER CBE

I must have done a good job with my foreword for the first Magpie Café Cook Book as it sold thousands and they've asked me back again to do this much awaited second book! I have absolutely no doubt that the success of that book was because of its wonderful recipes and great photos, but even more due to the great job that Ian Robson and his team do in consistently cooking some of the world's best fish and chips at the Magpie Café.

Fish and chips have recently had great PR due to the fact that they are a nutritious, value for money meal and are at the top of the British takeaway option outselling Indian food at a rate of 2:1. More people than ever have realised how good a meal fish and chips is and how good they are presented to the public especially in the North of England.

We are so lucky in our country that we land such great cod, haddock and other deep sea fishes even though many would argue that our government do nothing to encourage and help these heroic guys who regularly risk their lives to give us this consistency of supply. I am also convinced that the fish and chip shop industry is also grateful to the potato farmers of our country who provide such great stocks of chipping potatoes. Maris Piper, King Edward, Desiree and others are used to supply the 11,000 fish and chip shops in the UK.

For you of that way of thinking; did you know that more than 255 million fish and chip meals are sold every year and that if you laid all British potatoes that are turned into chips every year end to end they would stretch round the world 76 times?

So what does all of that mean as far as we are concerned? It means that we can still go and queue at the Magpie Café in Whitby and experience some of the best fish and chips in the world.

We can experience great service from smiling waitresses and have one of the best value meals time and time again. How I envy those who live near enough to get down to Whitby Harbour on a regular basis!

To finish I would love to wish the Magpie all the best for the future and paraphrase the great Madame Bollinger:

When we eat at the Magpie:

I eat at the Magpie when I'm happy
I even eat there when I'm sad
Sometimes I eat there alone
When with company for me it's a must
I trifle with fish and chips when I'm not hungry
But love them with salt and vinegar when I am
Otherwise I never eat at the Magpie
Unless of course when I'm in Whitby

Edited by: Martin Edwards
              Christopher Brierley

Design: Paul Cocker
              Richard Abbey

Photography: Jodi Hinds Photography
              www.jodihinds.com

Contributors: Linda Robbins, Andrew Coghlan
              www.sutcliffe-gallery.co.uk,
              Captain Cook Memorial Museum

Location accommodation from www.shoreline-cottages.com

First published in 2009 on behalf of:
Ian Robson – The Magpie Café
For additional copies of this book
in hardback or softback visit www.magpiecafe.co.uk

Published by:
Regional Magazine Company Limited
RMC House, Broadfield Court, Sheffield S8 0XF
Tel: 0114 250 6300 Fax: 0114 250 6320
www.regionalmagazine.co.uk

REGIONAL MAGAZINE COMPANY

TABLE OF CONTENTS

ACKNOWLEDGEMENTS

Thanks to
Chefs Marie Paling, Lou Middlemas and Jon Breckon for their help
testing recipes and preparing food for photographs.

To all our Staff, from Chefs to Kitchen Porters, Waiters to Cleaners
who all play their part, great or small, in making The Magpie what
it is today.

Brian Turner CBE for his freely given help and support.

Richard and Lynne Brewer and Family.

Dennis Crooks at www.crooksfish.co.uk

And all those who have given their time to help with
the editorial and pictorial content of this book.

Our customers who are the lifeblood of The Magpie.

And last but not least our respective wives Elaine Robson and
Lindsay Gildroy for putting up with a pair of workaholic chefs.

Dedicated to the memory of Margaret Dark

Sister, Colleague and Friend.

To many, for many years – the face of The Magpie.

THE MAGPIE FAMILY ALBUM

FROM THE ARCHIVES...

SOME OF THE PEOPLE, STAFF AND VISITORS ALIKE, WHO MAKE THE CAFÉ WHAT IT IS TODAY.

(SEE IF YOU CAN SPOT THE YOUNG LAD STANDING ON THE STEPS WHO IS CLEARLY ANXIOUS TO GET BACK TO THE KITCHEN AS HE'S A LOT OF BREAD TO BUTTER BEFORE OPENING TIME!)

MAGPIE CAFÉ

ABOUT THE AUTHORS

Ian Robson was born and still lives in Whitby with his wife Elaine. He worked in the plastics industry before making a life-changing decision to embark on a career in pursuit of his first love, good food.

Initially working for the then owners, he arrived at The Magpie in 1980. He continued to build on the Magpie's reputation and create the world-famous institution it is today. A quietly-spoken man by nature, he affirms that publicity and acclaim came looking for the Magpie rather than the other way around. He remains actively involved in the running of the café on a daily basis. His quieter moments are spent around the North Yorkshire coastline with his camera.

Co-author Paul Gildroy is the driving force behind the Magpie Café's 'engine room'. As head chef, he presides over the kitchens which produce food so good that diners will frequently queue for an hour just to sample it. After school in Whitby, he learned the catering trade in nearby Scarborough before returning to his home town, and its best-known restaurant. It was a return to familiar surroundings in more ways than one – Paul can claim an association with the Magpie Café dating back to the days when, as a 12-year old, he got his first job – buttering bread. His firm belief in allowing the simple natural flavours of good fresh ingredients to prevail, rather than detracting from them by complicated cooking techniques, has won over customers and critics alike. It is a consistent theme in the first Magpie Café Cook Book, which proved a huge success on its launch in late 2006. He lives with his wife and two young daughters in Whitby.

Ian Robson's Whitby...
FAMOUS SIGHTS

WHITBY ABBEY

The town's best-known landmark is the ruined 7th century abbey, which rises stark and spectacular from the East Cliff, at the top of 199 steps leading up from the town.

Built by Oswy, the Anglo-Saxon King of Northumbria, its founding abbess was Lady Hilda (later canonized), who presided over a double monastery of Benedictine nuns and monks.

The abbey later fell victim to a Viking attack and was abandoned for two centuries until being re-founded in 1078 under the orders of the Norman, William de Percy. This building survived for nearly 500 years until it was largely destroyed by Henry VIII during the Dissolution of the Monasteries.

It fell into ruin and much of the stone has since been carried off, but the site is now maintained by English Heritage – and its striking silhouette remains a prominent landmark.

WHALEBONE ARCH

This distinctive arch is a dramatic reminder of Whitby's history as a whaling port. Two centuries ago, women and children would climb up to this bleak headland to watch their menfolk leave for the icy north.

A fleet of more than 50 ships sailed regularly from Whitby at the heyday of the whaling industry, bringing back nearly 3,000 whales and attracting vital trade to the area. But there was a heavy price to pay too. In one of the worst maritime disasters, a catastrophic shipwreck 30 miles off the coast in 1826, some 200 mariners were lost, with only three surviving.

The original jawbone arch was erected around 1853 and is now displayed in the Whitby Archives and Heritage Centre. A replica was presented by Norway in 1963 and the current replacement was donated by Alaska in 2003.

ESK VALLEY RAILWAY

The Esk Valley line, running from Whitby to Middlesbrough, is widely regarded as a hidden gem of the rail network.

Starting from the historic station in the centre of the town, it runs for 36 miles through picturesque villages and unspoiled countryside, alongside the River Esk. Up to five trains a day leave the station – originally home of the Whitby and Pickering Railway, engineered by George Stephenson.

The line also connects with the North Yorkshire Moors Railway at Grosmont and there are trains from Grosmont to Pickering between March and November. Enthusiasts are currently campaigning for the link from Malton to Pickering to be rebuilt.

STEAM BUS

One of Whitby's best-loved inhabitants is Elizabeth, at 77 years old the world's only remaining three-axled steam bus. Even more impressively, she still runs a regular service from just a minute's walk further up Pier Road from the Magpie.

Elizabeth is run by Vernon Smith and his family, who bought her in 2003 as a flatbed wagon. The family fought to get a change in the Road Traffic Act so she could be licensed to carry passengers and, over the last few years, she has carried tens of thousands of them.

The Smith family are experts in the age of steam and have also driven trains on various television programmes. Vernon's most recent claim to fame came in the making of the Harry Potter films, in which he took the helm of the Hogwart's Express.

HEARTBEAT

To many television audiences, Whitby was a familiar backdrop for YTV's long-running flagship drama, Heartbeat.

Spectacular moorland scenery and 1960s nostalgia combined to keep the series at the top of the ratings, with audiences at around six million per episode.

The main filming location was actually the village of Goathland nine miles away, but Whitby itself has featured in many shows, doubling as the fictional town Ashfordly.

Ian Robson's Whitby...

THE GREAT,
THE GOOD
& THE SCARY

Photograph courtesy of www.sutcliffe-gallery.co.uk

Whitby may be synonymous with the Magpie Café, but it's not the only famous name associated with the town...

Cædmon's Cross stands near the abbey.

CÆDMON

One of Whitby's best-known sons was the Anglo-Saxon herdsman Cædmon, better known as England's earliest recorded poet.

According to 7th century theologian the Venerable Bede, Cædmon did nothing more remarkable than take care of the livestock at Whitby Abbey until one night he had a vision. In it, the work known as Cædmon's Hymn came to him and, from then on, he found he could sing and write inspirational verse based on the scriptures.

Encouraged by the abbess, Lady Hilda, he went on to become a devout monk and an accomplished poet, living out his days at the monastery.

MARY LINSKILL

Another eminent literary figure with Whitby connections is regional writer Mary Linskill, born in Blackburn's Yard in 1840. Her cottage has long since disappeared, but a plaque marking the spot can be found in a garden close to the top of the yard steps.

Mary left school at 11 and was an apprentice milliner before moving away to become a schoolteacher and governess. She later returned and settled in the neighbouring village of Ruswarp to concentrate on writing.

Her first success was with serial fiction, published in popular Victorian periodical Good Words. She then wrote a number of books including The Haven under the Hill – a name which is sometimes given to Whitby.

Mary's latter days were spent in Spring Vale, Whitby, where she died in 1891. She is buried in Whitby Cemetery and there is a monument to her in the parish church yard.

CAPTAIN JAMES COOK

Photograph courtesy of Captain Cook Memorial Museum, Whitby.

The 18th century explorer and navigator moved to the port of Whitby as a young man after setting his heart on a career at sea.

He became apprenticed to John Walker and his brother Henry, who were coal shippers – his first voyage was aboard the Whitby collier Freelove. Cook rose through the ranks and was duly offered command of a vessel at the age of 26, but instead chose to enlist as an ordinary seaman in the Royal Navy.

Within weeks he was promoted to master's mate, became Master two years later and eventually took command of his own survey vessel. After successfully charting the St Lawrence River and the coast of Newfoundland in Canada, he was promoted to First Lieutenant and undertook the three great voyages for which he is revered.

The first, in 1768, was as commander of the Endeavour, leading a scientific expedition to the South Pacific to observe the transit of the planet Venus across the sun. Cook was also given a secret mission to find the southern continent and he charted New Zealand and the east coast of Australia before completing a circumnavigation of the globe.

His second voyage of discovery was as Commander of HMS Resolution. This time he travelled from west to east, becoming the first man to sail round the world in both directions and the first to cross the Antarctic Circle.

Now a Captain, his final voyage was again in command of the Resolution, in search of the North West passage. En route he discovered the Hawaiian Islands and it was here that Cook met his death in a skirmish in 1779. His remains were buried at sea.

His achievements are commemorated, appropriately, with statues around the world: from Greenwich, London, and Sydney, Australia, to Canada, the Hawaiian Islands and, of course, on the cliff top in Whitby.

FRANK SUTCLIFFE

A pioneer of early photography, Frank Meadow Sutcliffe ensured that Victorian Whitby will live on for ever through his images.

Born in Leeds, Sutcliffe set up his first professional studio in 1875, in a disused jet workshop in Whitby's Waterloo Yard. He later established more salubrious premises in Skinner Street, developing his art and gaining an international reputation.

Sutcliffe's photographs were taken with cumbersome full-plate cameras of brass and mahogany, with a hand bellows. His glass negatives – 6.5in x 8.5in – captured the raw essence of Whitby and its surrounding area in a way that traditional artists could not.

His work won prizes in exhibitions from Japan to the USA, as well as in Britain. On retirement he became curator of the Whitby Literary and Philosophical Society and was made an honorary member of the Royal Photographic society in 1935.

LEWIS CARROLL

Alice in Wonderland - Lewis Carroll

Charles Lutwidge Dodgson, better known by his pen name, Lewis Carroll, was another regular visitor to Whitby.

He stayed in the town on seven occasions between 1854 and 1871, in the former Barnard's Hotel at number five East Terrace. The Victorian clifftop building, now La Rosa hotel and tearoom, bears a blue plaque marking its illustrious connection.

During his time in Whitby, Dodgson attended St Mary's Church and studied mathematics as part of a first class honours degree. A keen writer, he was also establishing a reputation as a raconteur and journalist and had a number of articles accepted by the Whitby Gazette. The first was a poem, entitled The Lady of the Ladle, which was set in the town.

But Dodgson was also working on ideas for his greatest work, Alice in Wonderland, and fellow mathematician Dr Thomas Fowler reported: "He used to sit on a rock on the beach, telling stories to a circle of eager young listeners... it was there that Alice was incubated".

His last visit was with other members of his family, in 1871, for his brother's wedding in the nearby village of Sleights.

BRAM STOKER

A bench, perched high on a clifftop above the Whitby coast, marks the spot that inspired what is probably the town's most enthralling claim to fame.

It was here that Abraham Stoker is said to have dreamed up the blood-chilling tale of Count Dracula's arrival, in the guise of a giant black dog, which leaps from a wrecked schooner off the storm-lashed shoreline. The idea based on the true story of the Demetrius, which had foundered on that very spot a few years earlier, discharging its grisly cargo of coffins and decomposed bodies into the sea.

The Irish theatre manager and author holidayed frequently in Whitby at the end of the 19th century, staying at the Royal Hotel. Sitting in the shadow of the ruined abbey, influenced by local folklore and the tales of the fishermen, he developed his concept for the Gothic horror story that would capture the public imagination from the time it was published in 1897.

Whitby forms a backdrop for three chapters of the book and Stoker's descriptions create a powerful picture of the Victorian town.

Ian Robson's Whitby...

TABLE TALK

Whitby people – and what they say about the Magpie

For Zoe and Michael Shardlow, the Magpie is very much a family affair. We regularly see not only them but their four children Matthew, Chris, Katie and Lilly … and now granddaughter Milly.

The Shardlows live four miles outside Whitby and run a tearoom and ice cream parlour where they sell ice cream made from fresh whole milk and double cream from local farms – some of which is on our menu.

They have been supplying The Magpie almost since they started their business 20 years ago. Michael makes the ice cream in a continuous freezer which turns out 900 litres an hour. There are about 30 flavours, all of them natural, ranging from rich vanilla to liquorice, whisky and ginger, Cointreau, orange and raspberry cheesecake and cinder toffee.

Kev and Tish Riley left Last of the Summer Wine country a decade ago to set up Whitby's first dedicated Goth guest house. They often nip over to the café from Bats and Broomsticks on Prospect Hill, which is in complete contrast to their own business. Their guest house is a haven for those who follow in the footsteps of perhaps our most notorious celebrity, Count Dracula.

Kev was a welder and Tish ran a children's clothes shop before they moved to the town, but as punks of the eighties and Goths, they already had an interest in all things dark and Dracula and that, together with their wish to live beside the sea, led them away from the rolling hills of Holmfirth to Whitby.

They spent a long time transforming what was a regular guest house into a mecca for the town's Gothic visitors. Now there are coffins, skeletons and spider's web four poster beds… indeed the couple have collected objets d'art from all over the world to the point where they have had to desist through lack of space.

"We get guests from all walks of life," says Kev, "from teenagers and their parents right up to an 80-year-old who came here to celebrate a birthday. People like something a bit different, and we enjoy providing it."

There's undisguised pride when solicitor Fred Richardson talks to other legal eagles throughout the country about his home town, especially when he tells them about The Magpie.

A retired partner and now a consultant in Thorpe and Co, Fred moved from Scarborough to Whitby with Diana, his wife of six months, in 1971, when he opened the firm's first branch in the town.

Over the years he has belonged to Round Table, 41 Club, Rotary and the local church. And in the days when Whitby was a thriving fishing harbour with more than 20 trawlers based here, he was heavily involved with the fishing industry as secretary of the local branch of the Keelboat Society. He's saddened that the change in European quotas has brought about the decline of the industry.

On the Magpie Café; "We have not seen it change a lot, it is still very much a traditional café which has always served – and still does serve – fish and chips par excellence.

"It's lovely to sit there and look across the harbour lights to the Abbey beyond – Diana and I regard ourselves as very lucky and privileged to have had a town like Whitby to raise our family, which has such great places like the Magpie."

  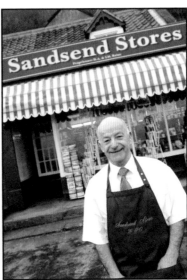

Everyone knows Dougie Raine; he's run Sandsend Stores just outside town for more than 40 years. It's more an emporium than a grocery shop – you can buy everything from a bottle of wine to a bucket and spade.

More recently he has spearheaded the campaign to raise £700,000 to provide state-of-the-art sports facilities for Mulgrave Community Sports Association in the wake of the disastrous foot and mouth outbreak which decimated the community.

"Everything was wiped out. I went to see Lord Normanby and we sat down together and decided we'd got to do something to put the community back together. One way of doing something was to build new sports facilities which everyone could use – and it would help in the fight against obesity."

The project was promoted by the Football Foundation as one of the best 'green' sports facilities around – using ground heat source pumps, special tiles on the roof for gathering power from the sun, a rain water harvesting system, top grade insulation – and 600 new trees have been planted.

It was officially opened by England and Newcastle United footballing hero Peter Beardsley and Lady Normanby a couple of years ago.

A former steeplejack, he has his roots firmly planted in Sandsend – he can trace his family back more than 500 years. It's a pretty hamlet with a population of around 200, that faces the sea, it's seen some pretty spectacular storms and flooding over the years. And Dougie, a retired coastguard, has witnessed them all from the shop, just a stone's throw from the beach. He gets up at 4am each day to sort the papers and, if Irene would let him, he'd spend each evening having dinner at The Magpie: "I've been going there for 45 years and I just love it".

As a high profile lawyer, who spends much of his time in the Old Bailey and other London law courts, Paul Bacon has a hectic lifestyle, so it comes as no surprise that in his off-duty moments he wants to relax away from it all.

In the 30 years that he and his wife Christine have been coming to the town, he's found that, when it comes to relaxation, you can't beat a leisurely stroll along the beach to Sandsend, and back, with their Westie, Sasha, followed by supper at The Magpie.

Nowadays the couple, whose son Richard is a popular television presenter, are adept at timing their visits to The Magpie to avoid the legendary long queues.

Ian Robson's Whitby...

SMOKE SIGNALS

It may not be as grand as the castle ruins, nor as quirky as the whale's jawbone, but there is one landmark in Whitby which draws just as many visitors.

To find it you must walk past the famous 199 steps on the east side of the river and follow your nose. It will lead you to W R Fortune's Smokehouse & Kipper Shop, an unpretentious building tucked away at the end of Henrietta Street.

The pungent aroma of smoking beechwood and oak leads to the distinctive red shop which bears a board telling visitors that the business was established in 1872.

And it's to this shop that staff from The Magpie Café go every day to buy the famous kippers, used in a number of dishes on the restaurant's menu.

Fortune's kippers are simply smashing. Our customers like them poached in the traditional way, but we also do kipper paté, kipper croquettes and fish cakes with kippers in them. And in our version of Cullen Skink we often use kippers instead of the usual smoked haddock.

You might say Fortune favours the early riser. With such an important ingredient it's no surprise that we, like other townsfolk 'in the know' make sure we go early to collect our kippers. Leave it too late in the day and you might miss out.

Fortune's is run by brothers Barry and Derek Brown; it was their great, great grandfather

who established the business in the days when herring was plentiful in local waters and there were quite a few smoke houses around. It was a seasonal activity carried out in the summer when catches were bountiful. In winter the men would find other work.

My first childhood job in the summer holidays was to collect barrow loads of boxes of kippers marked with one pair, two pair and so on from Derek and Barry's uncle Bill and take them back to my father's post office on Church Street.

I'd stick on the appropriate sixpenny postage stamps and then cancel the stamps with the Church Street Post Office ink stamp ready for the postman to take away. From that office, kippers by post would wing their way across the country. (None of your cardboard toy post office sets for me).

The smokehouse is still behind the shop. Its walls are thick with tar, a by-product of the burning wood smoke that envelops racks which hold not only the herrings, but bacon, salmon and haddock.

Barry and Derek have grown up with the trade. When they were small boys they'd spend time at the smokehouse lending a hand washing and cleaning and, as Barry put it: 'getting a feel of the place and a few bob in our pockets.'

When they left school they went into other jobs, but 16 years ago Derek came to help out his uncle in the business, followed a year later by Barry. Now they run the place.

Although the way in which the herring are smoked has changed little since great, great grandfather's day, a number of other things have. Since the North Sea herring ban, they have had to source their herring from elsewhere. They buy most of it from Norway these days.

The all-important 'fuel' is soft wood, beech and oak sawdust which comes from all over the country and beyond.

When the fish arrive they are gutted and cleaned and steeped in brine for 40 minutes before being hung in the smokehouse for around 18 hours. The smoking process colours the fish and preserves it, with the flavour dictated by the type of wood being used.

It's a technique which clearly fascinated filmmakers from New Zealand, who made a TV programme about Fortune's which has been transmitted in a number of other countries. The result has inevitably been regular visitors from Down Under, as well as Canada, Spain and elsewhere.

Soon Fortune's kippers could be available through mail order when a plan to put them on the internet comes to fruition – but there's no hurry. Fortune's has been around for well over a century. And it's not about to change just yet.

Ian Robson's Whitby...

THE FISHERMAN

There's a certain wistfulness about Richard Brewer as he nurses his mug of strong tea and gazes out across Whitby harbour. Richard is the sixth generation of fishermen in his family; he got his skipper's ticket when he was 21, the earliest age possible and he's been out there ever since. But now it's the turn of the next generation – sons Richard junior and Stuart – to take out the 106 tonne Copious, one of the biggest fishing boats working out of Whitby.

"It's a young man's job," he says "You just get too old for it – not mentally, but physically. I've found it hard to hand over, but it had to be done."

There is nostalgia, but, as Richard says 'there are no regrets.'

"I have made good deals and I have made bad deals, but I wouldn't change a minute. I have enjoyed everything: the people, the heritage, the odd-bods you meet. And I know so many people right from Scotland to the Cornish coast. I can go anywhere and I always bump into someone I know.

"Fishermen are a breed apart. We treat life lightly because it is such a hard job. There is death and there is poverty; there are good times and hard times, but we have to have a light attitude. You'd never see a fisherman stuck, you'd always help – you might expect him to buy you a pint when he gets ashore, but you'd never leave him stranded."

When Richard left school jobs were hard to come by – all the local boats at Whitby were fully crewed and he had to start at the bottom, but he learned quickly and qualified as soon as he could, which left him yearning for his own vessel.

"My wife Lynne and I scraped together all we could afford and we took our savings and our big ideas to a very big bank manager who agreed to lend us the rest to buy our first boat the Shulamit.

"I had to get out there and fish straight away. The first day I went to sea in that boat we had just £1 left between us in the bank and we had to leave it there to keep the account open."

As it turned out it was an auspicious week for the family – their baby son decided to be born as well.

"We started at rock bottom and built ourselves up – well there was only one way to go. Lynne helped in every way possible, physically and with the books, we wanted to build up something for the two lads. It's taken 30 odd years to do, but we are getting there."

The way we were... Fishermen like Richard Brewer
have inherited a tradition captured in the
photography of Frank Meadow Sutcliffe.
Photograph courtesy of www.sutcliffe-gallery.co.uk

They had the Shulamit for two years and it 'did OK'. As they could afford to upgrade they did so. One of the boats – and indeed the only one to undergo a name change – was the ill-fated Ocean Rose which was scrapped after a dangerous encounter with a chemical tanker. Some of the more superstitious locals thought there was something unlucky about changing the name.

"We were fishing quite legally about four miles offshore from Whitby when this tanker appeared. We couldn't move quickly because we were towing all our fishing gear and they hit us. The boat went through 90 degrees and I saw my young son disappear before my eyes."

Fortunately everyone survived and the foreign crew of the tanker were deemed to have been travelling too fast and were, according to the official report 'lacking in seamanship'.

Today fishing patterns have changed and the Copious is geared up to do whatever fishing is required – it could be eight to ten boxes or it could be 100 depending on the regulations. The 60ft twin-rig multi-steel vessel is equipped with the latest technology including a satellite computer which can send and receive emails and faxes.

There is a lot more mechanism which reduces the need to handle the fish making for a better product. Richard's team has been through the Responsible Fishing Scheme run by the Sea Fish Industry Authority, which guarantees that the product is as good as it possibly can be. The special stickers they are allowed to put on mean they can command better prices at market.

Their main catches are white fish – cod, haddock, whiting, plaice, lemon sole and monkfish and they have recently diversified into prawns. Their success is down to their local knowledge of areas, conditions and current fishing patterns as well as keeping their eyes and ears open.

It was Richard who first introduced The Magpie to a more exotic range of fish when he brought in some scallops and asked if we fancied cooking them. They were such a success that they launched a new era at the café.

And it was Richard who introduced celebrity chef Rick Stein to us too. He'd been doing a Tesco promotion in Whitby which required him to go to sea and The Copious was the boat chosen to take him. After a particularly stormy day on the ocean which saw the film crew

in a very sorry state, Richard suggested Rick went to The Magpie for his supper. That first visit forged a very special link between us – and the comment that the top chef had enjoyed the best fish and chips he'd ever tasted.

Now he's predominantly 'on shore' Richard is playing a leading role in the Anglo-Scottish Fish Producers' organisation which sorts out the fishing quotas for members and also represents the interests of the fishermen. He's been chairman of the organisation twice and a director since 1979.

He'll be spending more time with his daughter Toni Rose who is in her mid-teens, she works at The Magpie now but is desperate to go to sea, "She wants to become a female Rick Stein, so it's just as well she has access to just about any fish she could wish for."

Ask Richard what he loves about the sea and he'll come straight back: "Every darn bit of it."

"You see more of the nature of this planet when you are sitting aboard a fishing vessel than anywhere else. In the last year we have seen whales in the North Sea – we passed a pod and there must have been at least 90 minkys, basking sharks, porpoises and dolphins, just three or four miles out. Then there are thousands of beautiful sea birds…

"But you need to remember that the sea can change very quickly, and to know how to cope. I was never frightened, or even apprehensive or wary – you treat the sea with the respect it deserves. And if you feel frightened you have no right to be out there.

"You don't go out when the sea is rough, but it can turn rough when you are 17 or 18 miles from land; then there's nowhere to go and you just have to sit it out. You never put yourself or your crew in danger.

"In the winter it can be dreadful work, but in the summer when the weather is fine it's easily the best job in the world."

Ian Robson's Whitby...

TREASURES OF THE SEA

Ask a celebrity chef of Gordon Ramsay's reputation to name his favourite fish and chances are he'll choose something exotic like tipalia, served oven-roasted with mango and paw-paw salsa.

And who am I to argue? In this book, we've set out to present a world of different flavours, varieties, and ways with fish and seafood.

But for me it's tasty, meaty haddock – once an adventurous choice in the post-war days when it was the alternative to off-ration cod, but by today's standards, hardly exotic. To me though, there's nothing to beat it.

And lemon sole comes a close second – a completely different type of fish with a delicate flesh and a flavour of lemon, both of which are easily ruined by overcooking.

The daily list we chalk up on the blackboard at The Magpie gives customers a veritable shoal to choose from. We regularly feature the likes of skate, turbot, Dover sole, sea bass and John Dory.

What might have been a rarity on menus not ten years back is often commonplace – sea bass probably being the best example – it's a fish with its own distinctive flavour, and very popular. The same goes for monkfish, whose robust meaty qualities lends themselves to a lot of different applications. It is very good at absorbing flavours in dishes like curry, as it can take on the spice without being overpowered.

John Dory, is better known on the south coast than up here, but the catches are producing more and more of them. Probably something to do with global warming? Who knows. But given the opportunity I'd cook it whole on the bone with a nice light lemon sauce.

Salmon at The Magpie is mostly farmed organically these days. We do serve wild salmon, with its distinctive taste, but over the years we've been at the Magpie it's become harder to get hold of, not to mention more expensive. Organic farmed salmon is a lot better than it used to be and we can offer it at a good price.

The one species on the blackboard that always raises a laugh is woof. Nothing canine about this fellow though. It's actually another name for catfish, and I can best describe it as something half way between cod and haddock. It's also very versatile. Fry it, grill it, poach it – in fact anything you'd use cod or haddock for.

There was a time in the 1920s and 30s when tuna fisheries thrived on the Whitby coastline, but they were fished out of existence in the 1950s, and today tuna has to be brought in from much further afield. Other fish like gurnard and pollock are more plentiful in the seas locally, but they can't compete in the flavour stakes.

But if there's one thing that defines Whitby and the North Yorkshire coast in culinary terms, it's crab. Or more particularly, Whitby crab. They're bursting with wonderful, delicate, sweet flavours. Tastes and views vary as to how it should be served. Everyone has a different way of dressing crab, and each way is distinctive.

There are few eating experiences to compare with good dressed crab on its own. For me, it's superior to lobster, though it doesn't command the same status. That's a shame because personally I think lobster is overrated. Eating it is a lot of hard work for not a lot of reward and I don't think it's as flavoursome as crab.

However, there is lobster then there is lobster thermidor. It's the easy way to serve it, just the meat in a wine and cheese sauce.

Few varieties of seafood have enjoyed as much promotion by celebrity chefs over the last few years as scallops. So it's no surprise they are a great favourite at The Magpie. Customers who like to cook them at home often ask me for advice. If you're using fresh whole scallops rather than the pre-prepared supermarket variety, they are quite labour intensive to prepare but worth the effort. I prefer to keep the coral on.

When it comes to oysters, we look locally – up the coast to Lindisfarne – for ours.

Serve them still raw and chilled with a squeeze of lemon and a dash of Tabasco sauce. Or cook them in garlic butter, or as we do, tempura-style in batter. Check out the three ways with oysters in our recipe section.

The mussels on our menu are farmed in Shetland and best cooked the classic way in garlic, cream and white wine.

We have a notice in the restaurant which proudly proclaims that all our fish are sourced from well-managed fishing grounds to help with the sustainability of all our fish stock.

That's true – but it's also ironic, because I believe the problem with fish stocks today is that European efforts to preserve them have been largely misdirected, in my opinion they have gone about it the wrong way. I have been saying this for 20 years – if you restrict the landing, but not the amount that fishermen catch, good fish gets thrown back dead into the sea.

If the focus had been on increasing the mesh sizes in the nets then the small fish would have swum free and grown larger, then the boats would not have had to land as many to get the weight.

Why didn't they? Probably because of the expense of replacing all the nets – but that would not have been nearly as expensive for local fishermen as the outcome of the ruling.

But I'm a chef, not a politician and for now I'll stick to preparing the kind of dishes for which the Magpie is known. May you enjoy the treasures of the sea.

Ian Robson

A WORD ON WINES

It's fish for dinner – reach for the chardonnay! Hands up who's said that at one time or another? Thought so. But with just a little forethought you can enjoy food and wine so much more – and open up a whole new world of discovery.

Let's just take a little time to think about which wines suit which style of seafood. Oysters for instance require the freshness of a crisp Champagne or a classy Sauvignon Blanc such as a Pouilly Fumé or Sancerre, whereas fish with rich or spicy sauces could work better with a light red such as Fleurie, or a deep perfumed white grape variety such as Viognier. But how do we go about getting that right match?

A simple formula is to think about using the wine as one of your ingredients. By balancing the overall flavours on the palate it will help you enjoy these wonderful recipes with a suitable wine, while also taking into account your own personal tastes.

Here's a simple guide;

FRIED FISH

What, red wine with fish? Why not? The texture of fried fish is the gateway to some interesting choices. The oily texture from a batter gives the palate an additional coating and allows firmer tannin flavours to be absorbed. This opens up a whole list of wines to choose from, with my personal favourite being a Tarrango grape variety from Australia.

It's light red but with a good amount of fruit, at 14 per cent high in alcohol and with very good acidity which leaves your palate clean. Other good examples include red Burgundy, particularly from the Beaune, such as Hautes Cotes du Beaune and soft German red wines particularly from the Ahr valley or Wurtemberg.

The grape variety to avoid with batter is Chardonnay, which is oily in texture and therefore clashes on the palate.

SALMON

For dishes that involve roasting or pan-frying, look for a wine high in acidity and fruit, as you are matching to a fairly strong flavour. Riesling from the New World, particularly New Zealand, has a nice balance of fruit left on the palate. Generally the alcohol level will be marginally lower at around 11.5 or 12 per cent abv.

Riesling wines from the Mosel valley are also good although generally even lighter in alcohol at around 9 per cent. This slight sweetness marries nicely with the texture of the salmon so it's a winner every time for me.

But don't be afraid to experiment a little and try something different. Riesling is not fashionable now but 100 years ago it was the most expensive style of wine in the world, its price outstripping even red Bordeaux. The wines haven't changed but fashions have, and it just so happens that German riesling is currently out of favour. That just means that the wines are more affordable and better value than ever!

SMOKED FISH (COOKED)

It has to be a Viognier, the wild grape variety of the Rhone Valley with flowery perfume disguising a rich powerful and earthy finish. My favourite example at present comes from the sixth generation wine maker Juan Pablo Silva at the Casa Silva in Chile. This Gran Reserva packs a real punch and really stands up to smoked cooked fish with its slightly dry earthy finish yet balanced with a light summery perfume.

Why not try a dry Sherry, such as a traditional Fino? This can be a good match but with its power and alcohol it can be a one glass visit rather than a bottle. Tio Pepe can be a little sharp so try one of the traditional Solera Finos, for a softer approach.

OYSTERS

An easy match, this one. That beautiful fresh salty taste of the sea needs a contrast of green apple fruit and high acidity. In an ideal world, go for Champagne. My preference is for something grown in the Cotes de Blancs, the area south and east of Epernay where the Chardonnay grapes grow.

In the village of Le Mesnil Sur Oger there are two great producers. Krus Clos de Mesnil is a delightful 100 per cent Chardonnay Champagne from grapes grown in a walled vineyard, but there is the slight snag that it costs around £400 per bottle.

Nearby is the house of Launois. Here the seventh generation of the family makes Launois Blancs des Blancs NV which has white flowers and summer fruit on the nose with a crisp and tight acidic finish. Perfect with those lovely fresh oysters. And at around £25 per bottle it's not going to break the bank

As a still less expensive alternative, try a Menetou Salon from the Loire Valley. Crisper than a Sancerre and not as smoky as a Pouilly Fume, this up-and-coming village is really starting to make waves among Sauvignon Blanc wines.

PRAWNS AND LOBSTER

Sauvignon Blanc from Chile, preferably from Colchagua Valley, can be a great wine to go with freshwater prawns or lobster. Full of vibrant acidity, gooseberry and lime fruits and a delicious lipsmacking finish. Also try Vernaccia di San Gimignano from the walled city in Tuscany. Vernaccia is famously dry and historically the white wine of the Italian nobility. Michealangelo is reputed to have said of the wine " it licks, it stings and it bites". That's artists for you.

Good examples of Chilean Sauvignon Blanc start from around £5 at the supermarket but it may be worth trading up to a few pounds more to get something with distinctive flavours.

ON A
PERSONAL NOTE…

Don't forget, each person has a different palate for wines and what is right for me may not be right for you. If you like drinking heavy Claret with your fish and chips, or prefer drinking a glass of ale with your lobster, then these pages are not designed to discourage you. Just enjoy drinking with what you enjoy eating and I am sure that the world will be a better place for it. And after all, experimenting is part of the fun.

Andrew Coghlan

Andrew Coghlan is a north of England-based wine author and broadcaster with a special interest in matching techniques. His fully-illustrated book on how to get the best from food and wine, A Perfect Balance, was co-written with wife Janet. Enquiries; sales@wineschoppen.co.uk

A WORLD OF IDEAS

Just as Whitby once sent adventurers to far-off countries, our roots are firmly in North Yorkshire, but our cooking takes in influences from across the globe. Enjoy a selection from the Magpie Café's menu on the following pages.

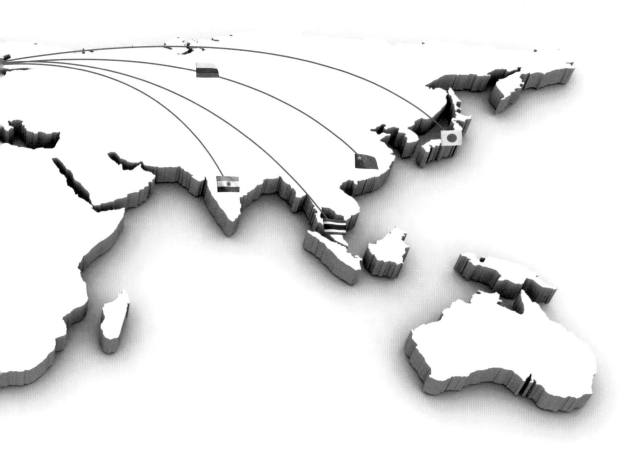

WHITBY KIPPER & POTATO SOUP

(CULLEN SKINK WHITBY STYLE) Serves four

INGREDIENTS

500ml fish stock

1ltr milk

2 large kippers

700g potatoes 1cm dice

4 shallots finely sliced

2 cloves of garlic crushed

100ml double cream

Salt and pepper

100ml crème fraîche

Chopped parsley to garnish

METHOD

Place all the ingredients (except the cream, crème fraîche, parsley and seasoning) into a pan and simmer gently until the potatoes are cooked. Remove the kippers and about half the potatoes. Skin the kippers and remove as many bones as you can. Gently flake the meat and set aside with the potatoes.

Using a stick blender, blitz the soup until smooth. Add the cream and salt and pepper to taste and return to the heat. Add the flaked kipper and potatoes to soup and warm through. Serve in soup bowls finished with a little crème fraîche and chopped parsley.

THE WHITBY KIPPER

First take your kippers – then follow our simple guide on cooking with this quintessentially British fish classic.

COOKING THE KIPPER

An easy way to cook kippers is to put water in a frying pan, bring it to the boil and place the kippers into the water. Cover with a lid and simmer for 4-5 minutes. Remove from the pan, pour a little of the water away, reduce the rest, and finish with butter then pour over the kipper and serve with brown bread and butter and a pot of strawberry jam. Eating the bread and jam after the kipper helps cleanse the palate ready for your next course.

You can also cook kippers in the oven. The method is similar to cooking them on the stove top. Put the kippers in a tray of water, cover with foil and cook in the oven for about 15-20 minutes.

Alternatively boil some water, pour it into a jug and stand the kippers in it. Leave for about 10-12 minutes.

Or simply grill them with a little butter, turning occasionally.

WHITBY KIPPER PATÉ

Serves four

INGREDIENTS

4 kipper fillets
4 shallots roughly chopped
2 cloves of garlic
150g butter
200g double cream
100ml white wine

Shot of brandy
Pinch of paprika
Juice of half a lemon
1 teaspoon of chopped parsley
Half teaspoon of chopped thyme
Salt and pepper

METHOD

Roughly chop the kipper fillets and place in a pan with the wine, cream, brandy, shallots and garlic. Gently poach the kippers for about five minutes. Pour the contents of the pan into a food processor and allow to cool slightly. Add the chopped herbs, lemon juice, paprika and blitz until very smooth, adding the butter a little at a time.

Alternatively pass the mix through a course sieve or a moulin.

Season to taste, place in ramekins and chill.

Serve with crusty bread with lashings of butter or melba toast.

MUSSELS WITH MERLOT, TOMATO AND PANCETTA

Serves four

INGREDIENTS

2kg fresh mussels cleaned with beards removed

200ml merlot

75g butter

6 shallots finely sliced

100g pancetta cut into lardons (small batons)

6 spring onions roughly chopped

400g tin of chopped tomatoes

100g cherry tomatoes cut in half

1 clove of garlic crushed

1 tablespoon of chopped parsley

METHOD

Melt the butter in a deep pan, and sauté the pancetta until cooked and golden. Add the shallots and garlic, cook until soft and translucent.

Wash the mussels. (**CAUTION:** if the mussels are open, tap them and they should close. If they don't close then throw them away).

Add the mussels to the pan with the tinned tomatoes and cherry tomatoes. Add the merlot and cover the pan with a tight fitting lid. Cook for 4-5 minutes, shaking the pan occasionally. Lift off the lid and check that the mussels have opened. If they haven't, cook for a little longer. This time, if the mussels do not open, discard and do not eat them.

To serve: share the mussels between four bowls, pour over the liquor and garnish with chopped parsley and spring onions. Serve with loads of fresh baguette to mop up the sauce.

KING SCALLOPS WITH TOMATO, GARLIC, BASIL & LEMON BRUSCHETTA

Serves four

INGREDIENTS

12 king scallops
Oil for cooking
For the bruschetta:
8 ripe tomatoes seeds removed
2 cloves of garlic
Half a red onion finely chopped
75g cucumber
Juice and zest of half a lemon
1 tablespoon of chopped basil
2 tablespoons of extra virgin olive oil

Salt and pepper
8 Slices of ciabatta
For the pesto:
75ml olive oil
1 teaspoon of pine kernels
1 small of clove garlic
1 tablespoon of chopped basil
A little parmesan
Salt and pepper

METHOD

To make the pesto: Lightly toast the pine kernels under the grill and put them into a food processor with the garlic, oil and basil. Blitz to a coarse purée and add a little parmesan and salt and pepper to taste.

For the bruschetta: Put the cucumber, garlic, juice and zest of half a lemon, olive oil and the tomatoes in a food processor. Blitz until coarsely chopped. Add the onion and basil, and salt and pepper to taste and blitz again.

Put the ciabatta slices under the grill and toast each side. Heat a little oil in a frying or griddle pan, slice each scallop in half, and quickly sear the scallops (no longer than 30-40 seconds each side).

To serve: Put some of the bruschetta mix on each of the ciabatta slices, then carefully place three pieces of scallop on each. Transfer to serving plates and drizzle with the basil pesto. Serve immediately.

WHITBY CRAB BISQUE

Serves four

INGREDIENTS

500g brown crab meat

200g white crab meat

1ltr fish stock

150ml white wine

400g tin of chopped tomatoes

50g butter

1 medium onion

1 carrot

Half a stick of celery

Half a leek

50ml brandy

100ml double cream

Salt and pepper

METHOD

Roughly chop the vegetables and melt the butter in a pan. Carefully add the vegetables and sweat them off without allowing them to go brown. Add the brown crab meat, wine, fish stock and tomatoes, stir well and cook for about 20 minutes. Using a stick blender, blitz the soup until smooth. Stir in the brandy, cream and flaked white crab meat. Add salt and pepper to taste and serve with lots of crusty bread

WARM LOBSTER & SAFFRON POTATO COCKTAIL

Serves four

INGREDIENTS

2 lobsters dressed

500g boiled new potatoes sliced

75ml white wine

Half a gram of saffron

2 shallots finely sliced

5 tablespoons of mayonnaise

75ml double cream

2 little gem lettuce

lollo rosso or oak leaf lettuce for garnish

Half a lemon

Oil for sauté pan

Salt and pepper

METHOD

Remove the lobster from the shell. Set aside the claws to be used for finishing the dish. Roughly cut up the lobster meat. Add the saffron to the wine to infuse.

Heat a little oil in a pan and add the sliced potatoes. Sauté until the potatoes have a little colour. Add the shallot and sauté a little more.

Add the wine, reduce a little, then add the lobster, cream and mayonnaise. Gently stir until the potatoes and lobster are evenly coated. Slice the lemon in half lengthways. Squeeze one half onto the lobster. Remove from the heat. Finely slice the little gem lettuce.

To serve: Using four wine glasses, layer the lobster with the lettuce starting with the lettuce and finishing with the lobster.

Place the lobster claw on top with a little bit of lollo rosso and serve.

SOUSED MACKEREL WITH WARM POTATO SALAD

Serves four

INGREDIENTS

4 large fillets of fresh mackerel

1 large onion finely sliced

8 peppercorns

1 lemon

200ml white wine

200ml water

2 bay leaves

Salt and pepper

300g new potatoes

3 tablespoons of mayonnaise

1 teaspoon of chopped parsley

1 teaspoon of chopped chives

1 teaspoon of chopped chervil

METHOD

Boil the new potatoes until tender. Drain and set aside to keep warm.

Place the onion, wine, water, peppercorns, bay leaves and half of the lemon in a large frying pan. Bring to the boil, reduce to a simmer and gently place in the fillets of seasoned mackerel. Cover with a lid. Cook for 4-5 minutes.

For the potato salad: If the potatoes are too large cut them up and mix with the mayonnaise and herbs. Add a little pepper if desired.

To serve: Place a spoon of the potato salad on each plate and carefully lay a fillet of mackerel on top. Garnish with a few dressed leaves.

SMOKED SALMON WITH ENGLISH ASPARAGUS & ENGLISH MUSTARD CRÈME FRAÎCHE

Serves four

INGREDIENTS

200g sliced smoked salmon
20 asparagus sticks
200ml crème fraîche

2 teaspoons of English mustard
Salt and pepper
Olive oil

METHOD

This is delicious – and really easy. Take each asparagus stalk, hold near the thicker end and bend until it snaps. This will snap the spear at its natural break point where the tender part of the stalk starts.

Lay the spears on a baking tray, drizzle with oil and season generously. Put into a preheated oven (200ºc or gas mark 6) for 6-8 minutes. Alternatively toss the spears in oil in a sauté pan. Mix the mustard into the crème fraîche.

To serve: Place five stalks per portion onto a plate, divide the smoked salmon into four, lay roughly onto the asparagus and pour on the mustard crème fraîche. Simple as that!

OYSTERS ROCKEFELLER

Serves four

INGREDIENTS

24 Pacific rock oysters

300g fresh spinach chopped (or fresh watercress, reputed to be in the original recipe)

Half an onion grated

Half a stick of celery grated

2 tablespoons of chopped parsley

2 slices of streaky bacon finely diced

1 tablespoon of finely chopped capers

2 tablespoons of olive oil

Juice of half a lemon

Splash of Tabasco

50g unsalted butter

50ml absinthe (Pernod will do)

3 tablespoons of fresh breadcrumbs

METHOD

Open the oysters, drain off the liquid and keep for later. Put the oysters in the fridge to keep cool.

Heat the oil in a pan and add the bacon, onion and celery. Cook over a medium heat until the bacon is cooked and add the capers, juice of the lemon, spinach and parsley. Add a few drops of Tabasco to taste.

Put in the absinthe in another pan and burn off the alcohol. Add the butter and whisk in. Add some of the oyster juice and reduce a little

Place the oysters on a tray (tip: to level the oysters put some table salt under them & sit the oyster on top), divide the spinach mixture between the oysters and pour over the absinthe liquor. Top with breadcrumbs and place into a preheated oven (220ºc) for around eight minutes. Remove and flash under the grill to brown the breadcrumbs and serve immediately.

OYSTER TEMPURA WITH ORIENTAL DIP

Serves four

INGREDIENTS

24 Pacific rock oysters
200ml sparkling water
100g plain flour
50g cornflour
2 egg yolks
Half a teaspoon of baking powder
Half a teaspoon of salt
Beef dripping or vegetable oil for deep frying

For the dip:
50ml soy sauce
1 spring onion finely chopped
Half a teaspoon of grated fresh ginger
1 teaspoon of honey
1 finely diced red chilli

METHOD

For the batter: Sieve the flour, cornflour, baking powder and salt into a bowl and whisk in the egg yolks and water until smooth and the consistency of double cream. Put in the fridge to rest and chill.

For the dipping sauce: Mix all the ingredients together and set aside.

Half fill a pan with the dripping and heat to about 175°c. Alternatively, to check if the fat is hot enough drop a couple of drops of batter into the fat and if they come straight back to the surface bubbling then it is OK to use.

Open the oysters, keeping the deep shells, and dip them in the batter. Deep fry, laying them gently in the fat one at a time. The oysters should take 1-2 minutes to cook or until the batter is nice and crispy. Drain them on kitchen paper and serve them in their shells with a pot of dipping sauce.

MACKEREL & SPRING ONION CROQUETTES

Serves four

INGREDIENTS

4 large fillets of mackerel

1kg peeled potatoes (King Edward or Maris Piper)

8 spring onions finely sliced

4 shallots finely sliced

1 egg

1 tablespoon of chopped parsley

Salt and pepper

For the pané

Plain flour

2 eggs

6 slices of white bread made into breadcrumbs

Dripping for deep frying

METHOD

Cook the potatoes in salted water until tender. Mash, then add seasoning, the egg, sliced spring onions and the chopped parsley. Set aside.

Poach the mackerel fillets in water with the shallots, salt and pepper. Once cooked, remove the fish and shallots from pan and add to the potato. Mix gently to make sure the fish is spread evenly. Leave to cool slightly. When cool enough to handle divide the mixture into eight and make into cylinder shapes.

To prepare the pané: take three separate bowls, put seasoned flour in one, whisk an egg in another and put breadcrumbs in the third. Taking the croquettes one at a time, lightly flour each, roll through the egg and then through the breadcrumbs. Chill while the dripping is heating. Using a deep pan filled no more than half full, heat the dripping to 175°c. Gently lay in the croquettes – cooking four at a time is best. They should take between 4-5 minutes. When they are golden brown put them on kitchen paper to drain.

Serve with tartare sauce and dressed leaves.

CRAB, LOBSTER & LEEK TART

Serves four

INGREDIENTS

For the pastry:
400g plain flour
100g butter
100g lard
1 egg
Splash of water
Salt and pepper

For the filling:
Half a cooked lobster
100g crab meat white & brown
1 egg
100ml milk
75ml double cream
100g washed & finely sliced leek
Knob of butter
Salt and pepper
Crème fraîche to serve

METHOD

To make the pastry: Sieve the flour and add a little seasoning. Cut up the butter and lard into small pieces and add to the flour. Rub the fat into the flour to form a breadcrumb texture. Make a well in the centre of the flour and crack the egg into it. Mix with the flour, adding a splash of water if needed to form a smooth, soft dough. Wrap in cling film and chill for half an hour.

For the filling: Sauté the leek in the butter. Beat the eggs, add seasoning, milk and cream and fold into the crab. Add the leek and set aside.

For best results bake the pastry cases blind (ie cook the pastry without filling). Grease and flour six 10cm tart tins (or a larger tart or pie tin). Line the tins, leaving the pastry hanging over the edge (this will be trimmed when the pastry is cooked). Cut six larger circles, or one much larger circle if using a single tin, from parchment paper (this is called a cartouche) and place in the tarts. Fill each tart with baking beans (or use uncooked rice or dried marrowfat peas to weigh down the paper). Cook in a preheated oven (210ºc or gas mark 8) for about 20 minutes. Remove the beans and cartouche and return to the oven for 4-5 minutes. Take out of the oven and allow to cool slightly. Trim off the cases. Only four tart cases are needed – choose the best and keep two as spares or freeze to use another time.

Share the lobster meat between the four tarts then ladle in the crab mixture. Place in the oven (180ºc or gas mark 6) for 25-30 minutes or until they are set. Take them out of the oven and let them rest for a couple of minutes before taking them out of the tins.

Serve with some dressed leaves and crème fraîche.

LINDISFARNE OYSTERS FLORENTINE

Serves four

INGREDIENTS

24 Pacific rock oysters
(we recommend Lindisfarne oysters for their clean
fresh taste – native oysters are very good but usually
more than twice the price)
250g fresh spinach
2 shallots finely sliced

75g butter
50g plain flour
500ml milk
200g mature cheddar
Pinch of Paprika
Salt and pepper

METHOD

To make the cheese sauce: Place the butter into a pan and melt. Add the finely-chopped shallots and cook until soft. Add the flour to make a roux (thick paste), cook until the roux starts to take on a sandy texture. Gradually add the milk, bringing to the boil after each time. When all the milk has been added, bring the sauce to the boil and cook gently for a couple of minutes to cook out the flour. Add 150g of the cheese, whisk in and check the seasoning. Set aside while opening the oysters.

Once all the oysters are open, take them out of the shells and place in a bowl. Keep the deep shells and place on a tray which will fit under the grill. Preheat the grill to full. In a pan add the 25g of butter and the washed spinach, put a lid over and lightly wilt the spinach. Remove from the heat and share the spinach between the 24 shells. Sit each oyster back into its shell and spoon over cheese sauce. Sprinkle the remaining cheddar onto the oysters and finish with a pinch of paprika.

Place under the grill and remove when the cheese is bubbling and golden. Serve immediately with toasted French bread.

AVOCADO CRAB MEXICAN STYLE

Serves four

INGREDIENTS

200g white crab meat

200g brown crab meat

Half an onion

1 red chilli

5g ground cumin

1 teaspoon of chopped fresh coriander

Oil

For the guacamole:

2 ripe avocados

1 red chilli de-seeded & chopped

Pinch of salt

Juice of 1 lime

2 spring onions roughly chopped

1 teaspoon of chopped coriander

1 tablespoon of oil

Soured cream & tortilla chips to serve

METHOD

For the crab mix: Finely slice the onion and dice the chilli (all, some or none of the chilli seeds can be kept in depending on how hot you like your food). Put a little oil in a pan and add the onion and chilli. Cook over a medium heat to soften. Add the cumin and ground coriander and cook for a minute or so. Remove from the heat and cool slightly before adding to the brown and white crab meat. Mix well and stir in the chopped coriander. Chill.

For the guacamole: Cut the avocados in half, remove the stone (keep for later) and the skin. Place in a food processor with all the other ingredients and blitz until it starts to appear smooth, but still retains small pieces of avocado. Transfer the guacamole into a bowl and push the stones into it (the stones help to keep the avocado from turning black).

To serve: Layer the crab mix with the guacamole in small rings, remove the rings and top with soured cream and serve with tortilla chips.

DEEP-FRIED CALAMARI WITH AIOLI

Serves four

INGREDIENTS

400g fresh prepared squid (washed and cut into rings, the tentacles rubbed under cold water to remove the cartilage in the suckers)

Plain flour for dusting

Salt and pepper

Beef dripping for best results or oil for cooking

For the aioli:

2 free range egg yolks

200ml light olive oil

1 teaspoon of Dijon mustard

1 tablespoon of lemon juice

2 cloves of garlic crushed

Salt and pepper

Dressed leaves to serve

METHOD

Gently warm the dripping or oil in a deep pan – the pan should not be more than half full. While this is warming make the aioli or garlic mayo. Whisk together the egg yolks, mustard and garlic. Slowly add a drizzle of oil. Whisk well again, then add another small drizzle of oil. Do this until about a third of the oil has been added, when you can add the rest of the oil in a steadier flow, whisking all the time.

Slowly whisking in the first third of oil helps to emulsify the egg. If, while adding the final two-thirds, the mixture becomes too thick, add the lemon juice, which should thin it down a little. If when all the oil has been added it is still too thick, add a couple of drops of water.

Season to taste and store it in the fridge.

Worried about using raw egg? Whisk the yolks over a bain-marie, when they reach 65°c, plunge the base of the bowl into cold water to stop the cooking process Remove and proceed as the recipe. Still in doubt? Buy a good quality mayonnaise and add crushed garlic.

When the dripping reaches about 175°c, lightly flour and season the squid and gently lay it in the pan. It will only take about two minutes to cook and is best done in two batches to ensure it is cooked evenly. Place on kitchen paper to remove excess dripping and season lightly with sea salt and freshly milled black pepper.

Serve on warm plates with a few dressed leaves and the aioli.

CRAB & PRAWN PROFITEROLES

Serves four

INGREDIENTS

100g white crab meat

100g brown crab meat

100g cooked peeled prawns

200g cream cheese

1 teaspoon of chopped chives

125ml water

60g butter

75g plain flour

2 eggs

Sweet chilli sauce to serve

METHOD

To make the profiteroles: Place the water in a pan with the butter, put over a moderate heat to warm the water and melt the butter. Bring the water to a rolling boil and add the flour. Beat to a paste with a wooden spoon. Keep over the heat while beating until the paste leaves the side of the pan. Remove from the heat and cool.

Preheat the oven to 210°c or gas mark 8. Once the mixture has cooled, beat in the brown crab meat and the eggs, one at a time. Put the mixture into a piping bag and pipe 16 gobstopper-size mounds onto a baking sheet. Sprinkle with water and put into the oven for about 20-25 minutes.

Bake until golden brown and firm to the touch. Remove from the oven and allow to cool slightly.

For the filling: Beat the cream cheese with a spoon to soften. Roughly chop the prawns and add to the cheese with the white crab meat and chives. Put the mixture into a piping bag.

Pierce a hole in the bottom of each profiterole and pipe the cheese mixture into them, filling generously.

Serve four profiteroles per person with a generous amount of sweet chilli sauce.

Best eaten on the day of making, but if made in advance the profiteroles can be 'flashed' in a hot oven and then filled with the crab and prawn mix.

MAGPIE FISH SOUP WITH POTATO ROUILLE

(BOUILLABAISSE) Serves four

INGREDIENTS

1ltr fish stock

750g tomatoes, skinned, de-seeded & roughly chopped

1 bulb of fennel

1 medium onion

3 cloves of garlic

Half a leek

1 tablespoon of tomato purée

Half teaspoon of saffron

1 good sprig of thyme

1 tablespoon of chopped parsley

1-2 fillets of gurnard (approx 200g scaled & boned)

1-2 fillets of sea bass (approx 200g scaled & boned)

1 fillet of monkfish (approx 200g skinned)

300g fresh mussels

200g fresh clams

8 raw king prawn tails shelled & de-veined

100ml vermouth

A little oil

For the potato rouille:

2 medium potatoes

2 cloves of garlic

1 red chilli

2 eggs

100ml extra virgin olive oil

Salt and pepper

Half teaspoon of chopped parsley

METHOD

To make the rouille: Bake the potatoes in the oven, when they are ready and still piping hot, scoop out the potato and put into a food processor with the eggs, garlic, chilli and salt and pepper Blitz until smooth. It is important to do this while the potato is hot to ensure that the egg is cooked.

When it's smooth and the food processor is still running, gradually add the oil until the mixture almost resembles mayonnaise. Chill.

To make the soup: Finely slice the onion, fennel, leek and garlic. Heat the oil in a deep pan, add the vegetables and sauté lightly. Add the vermouth, fish stock and saffron, tomatoes and purée. Bring to the boil, reduce and simmer. Cut the fish into eight pieces of each variety and add to the soup along with the mussels, clams and prawns. Cover and cook for 8-10 minutes. Remove the lid and add the chopped herbs. Check and adjust the seasoning. All the shellfish should be open (discard any that aren't) and the prawns should be pink

To serve: Divide the fish and shellfish between four large bowls and pour over the liquor. Serve immediately with lots of French bread and the potato rouille.

MAGPIE SEAFOOD PAELLA

Serves four

INGREDIENTS

300g paella rice

1 red pepper

1 yellow pepper

1 green pepper

1 large onion

100g chorizo sausage

Half a gram of saffron

100ml white wine

2ltrs chicken stock

4 king prawn tails shelled, de-veined & cut in two lengthways

4 king scallops sliced in half

100g fresh prepared squid sliced into rings

200g fresh mussels beards removed

100g fresh palourde clams

150g monkfish cut into eight pieces

4 tablespoons of olive oil

Chopped fresh parsley to serve

METHOD

Roughly dice peppers, onion and chorizo – into 1cm cubes. Infuse the wine with the saffron which will turn it orange and give it the scent of the saffron.

Heat the oil in a large shallow pan – preferably a paella pan since this dish is supposed to be served in the pan in which it is cooked. Add the onions, peppers and chorizo. Fry for a few minutes until the oils start to come out of the chorizo – this helps give the dish colour and a smoky flavour.

Add the rice, stirring it to again pick up the colours and flavour of the oil, and then add the saffron-infused wine. Reduce to a medium heat and gradually add the stock. The rice will absorb the stock as it cooks. Don't forget to stir the rice regularly to avoid it sticking to the pan. Continue this until you have added half the stock and then start adding the fish.

The monkfish and prawn tails should be added first with a little more stock. Stir in and cook for a couple of minutes. Stir in the rest of the stock and add the mussels, thick end down into the rice so they are pointing upwards. Scatter the kings scallops, squid and palourdes over the rest. Cover with foil and cook for a further five minutes.

Remove the foil and sprinkle over some chopped parsley. Serve immediately.

LOBSTER THERMIDOR

Serves four

INGREDIENTS

2 whole dressed lobsters (half a lobster per portion)

100g butter chilled & cubed

2 shallots finely sliced

100ml white wine

2 teaspoons of English mustard

300ml double cream

2 bottlecaps of brandy

80g mature cheddar cheese

1 tablespoon of oil

50g grated fresh parmesan

METHOD

Remove the lobsters from their shells. Place the shells onto a baking tray or oven-proof dish. Keep the claws separate from the rest of the meat.

In a pan, heat the oil and add the shallots and gently cook until slightly coloured. Add the wine, cream and mustard and then the meat from the lobsters to warm through.

Remove the meat and divide it equally into the lobster shells. Return the pan to the heat, bring to the boil and reduce a little.

Add the brandy and whisk in the butter a little at a time (this should help thicken and emulsify the sauce).

Finally, add the cheddar cheese and mix well. Pour the sauce over the lobster meat in the shells. Sit the claw on top, sprinkle with parmesan and flash under the grill until golden and bubbling. Transfer to a serving plate and serve with lightly-dressed leaves and sautéed potatoes.

KING SCALLOPS WITH PORK RISSOLES

(SAGE AND ONION BUTTER) Serves four

INGREDIENTS

12 king scallops

150g pork mince

Half an onion finely chopped

1 teaspoon of chopped parsley

Half a teaspoon of ground ginger

1 clove of garlic crushed

3 tablespoons of fresh breadcrumbs

1 egg

Salt and pepper

oil for cooking

For the butter:

125g butter

1 red onion finely chopped

1 dessertspoon of chopped sage

METHOD

For the rissoles: Mix together the mince, parsley, ginger, garlic and seasoning. Divide the mix into four, then divide each into three so you have 12 in total. With floured hands, mould into wheel shapes.

Heat a little oil in a frying pan and, over a moderate heat, add the rissoles clockwise into the pan (this is so you know which went in first when they need turning.) Cook the rissoles for $1\frac{1}{2}$-2 minutes and then turn.

In another pan heat a little oil and add the scallops clockwise. Cook over quite a high heat for about a minute each side. The rissoles should be cooked by the time the scallops are ready.

To serve: Place three rissoles onto each plate and sit a scallop on top of each. Put the pan in which the scallops were cooked back onto the heat and add the butter and red onion. Lightly cook the onion and add the sage. Spoon the butter over the scallops and serve immediately.

HALIBUT WITH BLUE CHEESE TOMATO & BASIL RISOTTO WITH CRISPY PANCETTA

Serves four

INGREDIENTS

4 x 250g fillets of halibut

150g blue stilton

250g carnaroli risotto rice

1 large onion finely chopped

2 cloves of garlic crushed

300ml passatta (sieved tomatoes)

1ltr chicken stock

100ml red wine Merlot or Cabernet Sauvignon

1 tablespoon of fresh chopped basil

200g cherry tomatoes

Splash of balsamic vinegar

Olive oil

8 thin slices of pancetta

Salt and pepper

METHOD

Make a deep slit into each fillet of fish. Lightly pepper inside the fish and press the cheese into each slit, pushing well inside. Close the opening, secure with a cocktail stick and set aside.

For the risotto: pour a little oil into a deep pan and lightly sauté the onion and garlic. Stir in the rice and add the wine and passatta. Gradually add the stock a little at a time, stirring to make sure it doesn't stick to the pan.

Crisp the slices of pancetta in lightly-oiled frying pan, remove from the pan and set aside. Gently lay the fish fillets in the pan flesh side down and cook for a couple of minutes. Turn the fish over and place into a preheated oven (220°c or gas mark 8) and bake for about ten minutes.

Put the cherry tomatoes on a baking tray and drizzle with balsamic vinegar and oil. Season well and place in the oven for the same amount of time as the fish.

When the fish and tomatoes are ready, check the risotto – the grains of rice should be soft with a light bite in the middle. Check the seasoning then fold through the tomatoes with juices and the chopped basil.

To serve: put a large spoonful of the risotto in a bowl and sit the fish on top. Finish with a couple of slices of pancetta on each and a sprig of fresh basil.

COD & PRAWN BURGER

Serves four

INGREDIENTS

400g raw king prawn tails shelled & de-veined

300g fresh cod

2 tablespoons of mayonnaise

1 tablespoon of Worcestershire sauce

Half a bunch of spring onion roughly chopped

1 teaspoon of chopped chives

Good pinch of cayenne pepper

Black pepper

1 clove of garlic

Zest of half a lemon

Oil for cooking

4 soft burger buns

Homemade tartare sauce (see sauces page 149)

METHOD

Divide the prawns in half. Chop one half roughly and set aside, place the other into a food processor with the cod and blitz until smooth. Add the mayonnaise, Worcestershire sauce, spring onion, chive, cayenne, garlic, lemon zest and pepper and blitz until evenly mixed. Transfer to a bowl. Fold in the chopped prawns and divide the mix into four moulding each into a wheel shape.

Heat the oil in a frying pan and gently set down the burgers. Cook over a medium heat, turning occasionally until they are firm when gently pressed, around 3-4 minutes.

To serve: Cut the buns in half and sit the burger on one half, garnish with lettuce, tomato and onion, and serve with lashings of homemade tartare sauce.

COQUILLES SAINT JACQUES

Serves four as a starter

INGREDIENTS

12 king scallops
100ml white wine
50ml fish stock
250ml double cream
125g butter

1kg peeled potatoes (a floury potato suitable for
mashing such as Maris Piper or King Edward)
Salt and pepper
Parsley to garnish

METHOD

Peel and chop the potatoes, place into a pan of salted water and bring to the boil. Cook until tender, strain and mash with the 25g butter and 50ml double cream and season to taste. Put in a piping bag and allow to cool slightly, enough to handle.

Pipe the potato around the edge of a large dish (approx 9in x 9in) or four individual dishes (approx 5in x 5in) and place under a preheated grill to brown.

While the potato is under the grill put the wine and fish stock into a pan and add the scallops. Cover with a lid and poach for a couple of minutes. Remove the scallops from the pan and keep warm. Bring the wine liquor to the boil and add the cream. Reduce a little and whisk in the remaining butter, remove from the heat.

Take the dishes from under the grill and place the in scallops (three per portion if using the smaller dishes) pour over the sauce, garnish with a sprig of parsley and serve.

PAN-FRIED HADDOCK WITH MEDITERRANEAN PASTA

Serves four

INGREDIENTS

4 x 300g haddock (thick pieces are better for pan-frying)

300g dried fettuccine

For the sauce:

1 large aubergine chopped into half inch dice

3 courgettes sliced

1 large onion finely diced

2 cloves of garlic crushed

400g tin of chopped tomatoes

300g cherry tomatoes quartered

1 teaspoon of chopped basil

1 sprig of thyme

75ml port

50ml water

Pinch of sugar

Salt and pepper

Oil for cooking

Extra virgin olive oil for drizzling

METHOD

Spread the courgettes and aubergines on a tray and lightly sprinkle with salt. Cover with cling film and leave for about 30 minutes. (This helps to draw out some of the bitterness). Rinse with cold water and dry off excess water with kitchen paper.

Heat a little oil in a large sauté or frying pan and add the onion, courgette, aubergine and garlic. Sauté until lightly coloured. Add the chopped tomatoes, water and port. Cook over a medium heat for about ten minutes or until reduced a little. Add the cherry tomatoes, herbs, sugar and seasoning and cook for a further five minutes. Season to taste and set aside to keep warm.

Bring a pan of salted water to the boil ready for the pasta.

Heat a little oil in a frying pan. Season the haddock and gently lay in the fish, flesh side down, in the pan. Cook for 3-4 minutes, turn the fish over and cook for a further 3-4 minutes.

While the fish is cooking, cook the pasta as instructed, strain and toss with the Mediterranean sauce.

To serve: Divide the pasta between four plates, lay the haddock (flesh side down) on top, drizzle with the extra virgin olive oil and serve.

THAI-STYLE SHELLFISH & NOODLE BROTH

Serves four

INGREDIENTS

12 king prawn tails

4 langoustines

100g queen scallops

150g cockles or clams

400g mussels

2 red chillies de-seeded and finely chopped

4 spring onions finely chopped

1 heaped teaspoon (or to taste) of grated fresh ginger

1 lemon grass stalk finely chopped

100g fine thread rice noodles

300ml white wine

600ml water

METHOD

Put the noodles in some hot water to soften and leave for 3-4 minutes.

Put the 600ml of water in a pan and add the wine, chilli, ginger and lemon grass. Bring to the boil and add the king prawns, langoustines and mussels. Cover with a lid and simmer gently for two minutes. Add the cockles, queen scallops and spring onion and cook for a further two minutes. When the prawns have turned pink and the mussels and cockles have fully opened (discard any which aren't), take half of the mussels and remove them from their shells. Place the strained, warm noodles in a bowl and add all the shellfish, pour over the cooking liquor and serve immediately.

WARM OAK ROASTED SALMON WITH POACHED EGG & HOLLANDAISE SAUCE

Serves four

INGREDIENTS

4 x 150g oak roast salmon (also called Bradhan Rost)

4 free range eggs for poaching

For the hollandaise:

2 free range egg yolks

2 tablespoons of white wine vinegar

8 peppercorns

Half a shallot very finely sliced

200g unsalted butter melted and kept warm

Salt to taste

METHOD

Put the salmon on a baking tray and place in a preheated oven (180ºc or gas mark 4) for about eight minutes.

For the hollandaise sauce: Put the vinegar, shallots and peppercorns into a small pan and reduce to a third. Remove from the heat, add a teaspoon of cold water and cool slightly. Add the egg yolks, whisking over a gentle heat until they are the consistency of thick cream and show the mark of the whisk. This is called a sabayon.

Add a steady drizzle of warm butter, whisking continuously until the all butter is used. This requires patience – adding the butter too quickly will split the sauce. If this does happen, add half a teaspoon of hot water to bring it back together, then carry on.

When all the butter has been added, pass the sauce through a sieve and keep warm.

To poach the eggs: Bring a deep pan of lightly salted water to the boil and add a couple of splashes of malt vinegar. Reduce the heat to soft boil and add the eggs one at a time. Poach for about three minutes, remove from the pan and drain on kitchen paper.

To serve: Place a piece of fish on each plate, sit the poached egg on top of the fish and spoon over hollandaise sauce. Serve immediately.

PIZZA DOUGH CALZONE WITH SCALLOPS, MUSSELS & PROSCIUTTO HAM

Serves four

INGREDIENTS

For the pizza dough:
250g white bread flour
1 teaspoon of salt
7g dried yeast (or 15g fresh)
1 tablespoon of olive oil
Warm water

For the calzone:
1 batch of pizza dough
600g grated mozzarella
200g queen scallops raw
400g live mussels (to cook – 100ml white wine, knob of
butter, 1 garlic clove crushed)
4 shallots finely sliced
100g mushrooms finely sliced
30g butter
4 slices of prosciutto ham
300ml passatta

METHOD

Sieve the flour and salt into a bowl and add the yeast. Make a well in the flour and add the oil and most of the water. Work the flour into the water with your fingers adding the rest of the water if needed to form a slightly sticky dough.

Tip the dough out onto a well floured surface and knead for about ten minutes, when the dough should be really smooth. Put into a well-greased bowl, cover with a warm damp towel and leave in a warm place to prove and double in size.

Once it has doubled remove it from the bowl and knead the dough for a further minute to disperse any large bubbles of air. The dough is now ready for use.

Steam the mussels in the wine, garlic and butter until they open, discarding any that don't. Remove them from their shells and set aside.

Sauté the mushroom and shallots in the butter until they are lightly coloured and set aside.

Divide the dough into four and roll each piece into thin round discs.

Place a little cheese just off centre of each disc, then share the queen scallops, mussels, mushrooms and shallots between the four, cover with the rest of the cheese and lay a slice of prosciutto ham over each.

Dab water around the edge of each pizza and fold over the dough to form a pasty and nip the edges. Place on a baking sheet cook at 220ºc or gas mark 8 for 15-18 minutes or until the calzone looks golden and puffed.

Heat the passatta, plate up your calzones and pour over the hot passatta and sprinkle with freshly torn basil leaves.

PAN-SEARED TUNA & SWEET SPICY NOODLES WITH PORK & PRAWN SPRING ROLLS

Serves four

INGREDIENTS

4 x 200g fresh tuna

500g dried medium egg noodles

300ml water

300g sugar

1 tablespoon of tomato ketchup

1 tablespoon of white wine vinegar

3 red chillies finely chopped and seeds removed

8 spring roll sheets

200g pork mince

1 tablespoon of soy sauce

6 king prawn tails roughly chopped

2 spring onions finely chopped

2 pak choi finely sliced

100g sugar snap peas cut in half

Oil for stir frying

Salt and pepper

METHOD

To make the chilli sauce: Place the chillies, water, sugar and vinegar into a pan and boil until syrupy. Remove from the heat and stir in the tomato ketchup.

To make the spring rolls: Season the pork mince and cook in a little oil. Add the soy sauce, remove from the heat and cool a little. Fold in the chopped raw prawns and spring onion. Share the mix between the eight spring roll sheets, roll into cylindrical shapes and seal with a little egg. Deep fry or oven bake until golden in colour. Deep frying should take between 5-6 minutes at 170ºc; oven cooking at 190ºc should take between 12-14 minutes.

Boil the noodles, strain and refresh under cold water.

Season the tuna. Heat a little oil in a frying pan, and cook the tuna for about two minutes on each side. This will keep the tuna pink in the middle.

Heat some more oil in a separate pan and sauté the sugar snaps and pak choi. Add the noodles and enough chilli sauce to coat the noodles.

To serve: Share the noodles between four plates, slice the tuna and arrange the pieces over the noodles. Finish with two spring rolls and sprigs of fresh herbs.

HADDOCK WITH QUEEN SCALLOPS & SPINACH PIE

Serves four

INGREDIENTS

800g fresh haddock (skinless and cut into 5cm squares)

400g queen scallop meat

160g washed baby spinach

100ml fish stock

200ml chardonnay

400ml double cream

60g butter

30g gluten-free flour

1.5kg floury potatoes
(Maris Piper, King Edward or Marquis)

Salt and pepper

METHOD

Boil the potatoes in salted water, strain, and mash with 100ml of double cream and 30g butter. Season to taste. Set aside.

Place the haddock in a pan with the fish stock and chardonnay and poach for about two minutes. Add the queen scallops and poach for a further minute.

Place the spinach in a dish 30cm x 20cm dish. Remove the fish and scallops from the pan, retaining the liquor, and place on top of the spinach.

Return the pan containing the liquor to the heat and add the rest of the cream.

Mix the flour and butter together to make a smooth paste or 'beurre maniere'. Whisk the paste into the liquor and stir over a medium heat until the mixture thickens. Season and pour over the fish and spinach.

Top with the mash potato and place under a grill or in the oven until golden brown. Serve immediately.

CURRIED PRAWN TAILS WITH NAAN BREAD

Serves four

INGREDIENTS

For the curry:
32 large king prawn tails shell off and de-veined
2 large onions
2 x 400g tins of chopped tomatoes
15g black mustard seeds
5g ground chilli (10g if you like it very hot)
15g ground coriander
5g garam masalla
10g curry leaves
10g ground cumin
5g garlic salt
Three-quarters of a pint of double cream
1 tablespoon of chopped fresh coriander
2 tablespoons of oil

For the naan bread:
600g white bread flour
1 teaspoon of salt
15g fresh yeast (or 1 x 7g packet fast action dried yeast)
2 eggs
4 tablespoons of natural yogurt
8 tablespoons of warm milk
2 tablespoons of oil
Butter for brushing

METHOD

To make the naan: Sieve the flour and salt into a bowl and make a well in the centre. Whisk the eggs and add them to the flour with the yogurt and oil. Put the fresh yeast in the warm milk to dissolve and add this to the flour. Mix together to form a soft dough and knead for about ten minutes. Return to the greased bowl and prove for about 30 minutes (or until doubled in size).
Preheat a baking sheet in a hot oven (220°c or gas mark 8). Once the dough has doubled in size, knead it to knock out all the big bubbles of air, split into eight and roll each one into a flat teardrop shape. Place onto the baking sheet and brush generously with melted butter. Place in the oven and bake for 5-6 minutes, turning once.

To make the curry: Purée the onions, heat the oil in a pan and add the mustard seeds, chilli, ground coriander, garam masalla, cumin, garlic salt and curry leaves. Let the spices cook gently for a minute then add the puréed onion and cook until gently for about 5-10 minutes. Add the prawns, tomatoes and cream, bring to the boil and simmer for about 15 minutes. Finish with the chopped coriander and a little more cream if the consistency is too thick.
Serve with pilau rice and the freshly cooked naan breads.

VEGETARIAN LENTIL PIE

Serves four

INGREDIENTS

500g Puy lentils

1 large onion roughly chopped

500g button mushrooms quartered

4 sticks of celery chopped

2 medium red peppers chopped

2 cloves of garlic crushed

2 x 400g tins of chopped tomatoes

1ltr vegetable stock

2 tablespoons of oil

Salt and pepper

1.5kg potatoes

50g butter

75ml milk

200g grated cheddar

METHOD

Heat the oil in a deep pan. Add the onion, celery, mushroom and pepper and sauté gently for 10 minutes. Add the lentils, chopped tomatoes and vegetable stock, bring to the boil and add the pepper – no salt at this stage as it prevents the lentils from softening. Reduce to a simmer and cook for about an hour. After an hour season with salt to taste.

Boil the potatoes in salted water until tender, strain and mash with the butter and milk, check the seasoning and adjust as required.

Pour the lentils into an oven proof dish (approx 30cm x 20cm) and, using a potato ricer, rice the potatoes onto the lentils. Finish with the grated cheddar. Place into a preheated oven (180ºc or gas mark 4) for about 40-45 minutes and serve.

ENGLISH PEA, ASPARAGUS & LEMON RISOTTO

Serves four

INGREDIENTS

300g carnoroli risotto rice

1.2ltrs vegetable stock

2 cloves of garlic crushed

100ml dry white wine

Zest of 2 lemons

20 asparagus spears

200g fresh peas

1 medium onion finely sliced

Salt and pepper

Oil for cooking

Rocket to garnish

METHOD

Heat a little oil in a pan and add the onion and garlic. Cook with a little colour then add the rice and white wine. Add the stock a little at a time stirring often, and allowing the stock to be absorbed into the rice.

Continue until most or all the stock has been absorbed or the rice is tender with a little bite in the centre.

To prepare the asparagus: Take each spear and bend a third of the way up from the thick end, allowing the spear to snap at its natural breaking point.

Heat a little oil in a pan and add the asparagus. Sauté until the spears have taken on a little colour.

Put 12 to aside for garnish, and the chop the rest roughly and add to the risotto with the peas and lemon zest. Cook for a minute to cook the peas, adding a little more stock or water if the rice becomes too thick and gloopy. Season to taste.

To serve: Share the risotto between four dishes and garnish with the asparagus and rocket. Squeeze a little lemon juice over just before serving.

WILD MUSHROOM & BUTTERBEAN STROGANOFF

Serves four

INGREDIENTS

600g wild mushrooms (like chanterelles, porcini, pine or slippery jacks. Exotic or dried mushrooms can also be used. For dried, take 200g, soak to re-hydrate and squeeze out excess water before use)

1 large onion finely sliced

2 cloves of garlic crushed

50ml brandy

400g crème fraîche

400ml double cream

Juice of half a lemon

50g butter

Pinch of paprika

1 tablespoon of chopped parsley

1 tablespoon of chopped tarragon

400g tin of butterbeans strained and rinsed

200g long grain rice

100g wild rice

Salt and pepper

Sprigs of fresh tarragon for serving

Oil for cooking

METHOD

Cook the rice in boiling water as instructed.

Heat some oil in a large frying pan and add the butter then sauté the onion and garlic, until lightly coloured. Remove from the pan. Add a little more oil and sauté the mushrooms over a high heat to gain colour then return the onion and garlic to the pan. Take the pan off the heat and add the brandy very carefully because it may flare up. Return the pan to the heat and add the crème fraîche and cream. Bring to the boil to reduce slightly. Add the juice of the lemon, chopped parsley, chopped tarragon and butterbeans and season and taste.

To serve: Strain the rice, share between four plates. Spoon on the mushroom stroganoff and garnish with sprigs of fresh tarragon and a pinch of paprika. Serve immediately.

SALMON WELLINGTON

(WITH WILD MUSHROOMS) *Serves four*

INGREDIENTS

4 x 175g salmon fillets (skinless and all of equal size)
400g puff pastry
50g butter
1 egg for washing
For the farce:
200g raw king prawn tails
100g white fish (whiting or cod)
1 clove of garlic crushed
1 dessert spoon of chopped parsley
1 dessert spoon of chopped chives

1 dessert spoon of breadcrumbs
Juice and zest of half a lemon
Salt and pepper
For the mushrooms:
200g wild mushrooms
1 clove of garlic crushed
50g butter
1 dessert spoon of fresh tarragon leaves
Pepper

METHOD

To make the farce: Place the prawns, fish, garlic and butter into a food processor and blitz until fairly smooth. Add some seasoning, the juice and zest of the lemon and the breadcrumbs. Blitz to combine. Add the chopped parsley and chives, mix well and leave to rest.

Roll out the pastry, to an approx 30cm square, then cut into four. Brush each piece of salmon with softened butter and season with salt and pepper.

Spread the farce evenly on the top side of each piece of salmon, turn the salmon over and place onto the pastry, slightly off centre. The shorter edge of pastry should cover the side of the salmon and the longer edge should wrap around to meet the shorter side.

Seal the pastry with a little water and trim any excess pastry to make a neat parcel. Turn the parcels over so the join is underneath. Prick a couple of holes in the top and brush with beaten egg. Place on a large baking tray, leaving 2-3cm between each parcel.

Place into a preheated oven (200°c or gas mark 6) for about 15 minutes or golden brown.

For the mushrooms: Melt the butter in a sauté pan, add the garlic and the mushrooms, and sauté until golden. Finish with the tarragon and pepper.

To serve: Place some creamy mashed potato onto each plate, sit the Wellingtons on the mash and spoon on the mushrooms.

FRESH-SEARED TUNA, MOZZARELLA & TOMATO

Serves four

INGREDIENTS

4 x 150g fresh tuna (thick pieces cut into two)

2 balls of fresh buffalo mozzarella

2 large ripe tomatoes

2 sprigs of fresh basil

1 clove of garlic

Extra virgin olive oil

Salt and pepper

METHOD

Slice each tomato into four, discarding the top or bottom and lightly season. Slice the mozzarella into four and set aside with the tomato.

Heat up a frying pan or griddle. Slice the garlic in half and use it to rub the tuna. Season with salt and pepper. Lightly oil the pan and gently place in half the tuna. Sear on a high heat for about 30 seconds on each side, so that the tuna is nicely brown on the outside but still pink on the inside.

Repeat with the other pieces of tuna. While they are cooking, start to build the stack. Start with a piece of tuna, then a slice of mozzarella, followed by a slice of tomato. Repeat this again and finish with fresh torn basil leaves and a drizzle of good extra virgin olive oil. Do the same with the other pieces of tuna and serve immediately as a starter or as a light lunch with crispy sautéed potatoes.

POACHED COD WITH PARSLEY SAUCE

(A BRITISH CLASSIC) Serves four

INGREDIENTS

4 x 300g fillets of cod skinned & boned

4 shallots finely sliced

50g anchovy fillets

150ml fish stock

500ml full cream milk

200ml double cream

Salt and pepper

2 tablespoons of chopped fresh parsley

50g plain flour

50g butter

METHOD

Place the shallots and anchovies on the bottom of a pan or deep tray large enough to hold all four pieces of fish. Lay the fish on top and season with salt and pepper. Pour in the fish stock, milk then cover with a lid or foil, place over a low heat and gently simmer until the fish is cooked. The fish should look white, will feel firm to the touch and will flake easily. Remove the fish and keep warm.

To make the sauce: Put the milk back onto the heat and add the cream. Mix the butter and flour together to form a paste – this is what we call a buerre maniere or uncooked roux. When the milk is hot, whisk in the flour paste and slowly bring to the boil and simmer for a minute to cook the flour. Add the chopped parsley and season to taste..

To serve: Place each fish onto a plate and carefully pour over the sauce. Serve with new potatoes and seasonal vegetables.

PAN-SEARED SEA TROUT WITH BABY LEAF & SUGAR SNAP SALAD

Serves four

INGREDIENTS

4 x 250g fillets of sea trout

300g baby leaves (spinach, lambs, chard, rocket etc)

150g sugar snaps

300g crème fraîche

2 shallots finely diced

1 tablespoon of fresh mint chopped

Juice of half a lime

Oil for pan frying

Salt and pepper

For the vinaigrette dressing:

60ml extra virgin olive oil

30ml white wine vinegar

Juice of half a lemon

Salt and pepper

METHOD

For the vinaigrette: put all the ingredients in a jar and shake vigorously until combined. Wash the leaves and sugar snaps, toss together and put aside.

Mix the crème fraîche, lime juice, shallots and mint together, set aside with the leaves.

Heat some oil in a pan, and gently lay the seasoned trout in the pan, flesh side down. Fry for about two minutes until golden. Turn the fish over and fry for a further 3-4 minutes turning the heat down to moderate after two minutes.

To test if the fish is cooked, press it lightly. It should feel quite firm with a little spring to it.

To serve: Toss the leaves and sugar snap with the vinaigrette and place on the plates. Carefully remove each piece of fish from the pan and lay partly over the leaves. Finally spoon some of the mint crème fraîche over and serve immediately.

MAGPIE CARIBBEAN FUDGE

Serves twelve

INGREDIENTS

For the fudge:

200g dried mixed fruit

60g dried pineapple pieces finely chopped

60g dried papaya finely chopped

2 medium size bananas

100g dark 70% chocolate

100g hazelnuts crushed

75ml dark rum

200g butter

200g dark brown sugar

350g digestive biscuits broken

For the topping:

500g cream cheese

250g white chocolate

200ml double cream

50ml Tia Maria

METHOD

For the fudge: Line a standard swiss roll tray (approx 9in x 12in) with grease proof paper. Mash the banana with the rum. Melt the butter in a pan, add the dark brown sugar and stir until blended together. Add the banana mix, dried fruit, dark chocolate, hazelnuts and finally the digestive biscuits. Mix well and pour into the lined tray. Gently press it into the tray with a spoon, spreading evenly. Leave to cool before adding the topping.

For the topping: Soften the cream cheese with the Tia Maria. Heat the cream (do not boil) and add it to the white chocolate. Mix until the chocolate has melted, then add it to the cheese mix. Spread over the fudge and put in the fridge to set. Cut into 12 portions.

To serve: Smother each piece with whipped cream, fresh fruit and nuts.

MAGPIE SUMMER PUDDING

Serves eight

INGREDIENTS

500g brioche sliced

400g raspberries

400g blackberries

400g blueberries

300g strawberries

Juice and zest of 2 lemons

Juice and zest of 2 oranges

200g caster sugar

200ml water

1 vanilla pod

METHOD

Place all the fruit into a pan with the juice and zest of the oranges and lemons, the sugar, water and the vanilla pod which has been split with the seeds removed. Gently poach the fruit until soft. Remove from the heat and allow to cool slightly.

Cut a piece of brioche to fit in the bottom of a four pint bowl. Dip into the juices of the fruit and place into position. Then, using full slices repeat the process with the rest of the brioche until you have covered all of the bowl evenly up to the rim. Overlap the slices a little as you work to the top of the dish.

Remove the vanilla pod from the fruit. Add the fruit to the bowl and press it down firmly. Once all the fruit has been added place the last piece of brioche, dipped in the juice, on top to seal the pudding.

Pour any remaining juice over the pudding and place a plate on top.

Put a heavy object onto the plate to keep the pudding in place and pop it into the fridge for a few hours or preferably overnight.

To remove from the dish: take a flexible knife or pallete knife and push it down between the bread and bowl and loosen gently.

Place a large serving plate on top of the bowl and turn both upside down. Gently lift off the bowl. Serve with vanilla ice cream.

ENGLISH EGG CUSTARD TARTS

Serves six

INGREDIENTS

For the pastry:
250g plain flour
125g butter
60g caster sugar
1 egg

For the custard:
400ml full cream milk
4 eggs
50g caster sugar
Vanilla extract
Nutmeg to finish

METHOD

To make the pastry: Sieve together the flour and sugar, rub in the butter until the mixture resembles breadcrumbs. Whisk the egg and mix with the flour etc to form a dough. Wrap and leave to rest for about an hour.

Preheat the oven to 200ºc or gas mark 6. Grease six 100ml tart tins. Roll out the pastry and line each tin, place a cartouche in and fill with baking beans. Bake blind for about 20 minutes. Remove the cartouche and beans sand if necessary allow the pastry to dry off a little in the oven. Reduce the oven temp to 180ºc or gas mark 5.

For the egg mixture: Beat the eggs with the sugar and vanilla. Pour in the milk and divide the mix into the tarts. Lightly sprinkle ground nutmeg on the top of each tart.

Carefully place the tarts into the oven and bake until the custard is set. If it looks as though the tarts are browning on top, place them on a lower shelf and turn down the heat. Leave to cool to room temperature before removing from the tins.

Serve the tarts on their own or with a little fruit compote.

MAGPIE TREACLE TART

Serves eight to twelve

INGREDIENTS

For the pastry:
400g plain flour
200g butter
100g caster sugar
1 egg
1 egg yolk
drop of water

For the filling:
400g fresh white breadcrumbs
1100g golden syrup
1 tablespoon of black treacle
Zest and juice of 1 lemon
3 eggs
50ml double cream

METHOD

To make the pastry: Place the flour, sugar and butter into a food processor and blitz until the mixture resembles breadcrumbs. Turn off the machine and add the egg and egg yolk. Blitz again using the pulse button and add a little water to help to bind and form a dough. Do not overwork the pastry as this can make it shrink while baking.

To make the pastry without using a food processor, sift the flour into a bowl add the sugar and butter and rub in until the mixture resembles breadcrumbs. Add the egg, egg yolk and a little water, mix to form a dough.

Wrap the pastry and leave to chill in the fridge for about an hour before rolling.

To make the filling: Warm the syrup, add to all the other ingredients and mix well. Set aside while the pastry is rolled and baked.

Grease a 10 inch tart or flan tin. Roll out the pastry so it is a least 16 or 17 inches across, drape it over the rolling pin and gently place over the tin, lifting and pressing into the edges. Leave some pastry hanging over the sides – this will be trimmed after it has been baked blind. Preheat the oven to 200ºc or gas mark 7. Make a cartouche – parchment paper, cut larger than the item to be baked, put on top of the pastry and fill with baking beans or dried peas or rice, which helps to prevent the pastry from rising during cooking.

Bake for between 35-45 minutes, removing the cartouche five minutes before the end to ensure the pastry is not soft or wet. Remove from the oven and pour in the syrup mix Reduce the oven temp to 175ºc or gas mark 6. Return the tart to the oven and bake for approx one hour or until the filling is firm to the touch and a nice golden colour.

Leave to rest for about 30 minutes before cutting, then serve with lashings of thick clotted cream.

TRINITY CREAM

(THE FRENCH CALL IT CRÈME BRULÉE) Serves six

INGREDIENTS

600ml double cream

125g golden caster sugar

3 eggs

2 egg yolks

25g butter

100g demerara sugar for the caramel top

METHOD

Gently warm the cream in a pan over a low heat. Mix the sugar, eggs and egg yolks together in a bowl. Heat the butter in another pan until it bubbles and foams, just as it starts to brown. The butter should be a dark tan colour similar to a hazelnut, hence the name 'nut brown butter or beurre noissette'. When it gets to this stage it will quickly turn from brown to black so keep a watchful eye on it.

Pour the butter into the cream and the cream onto the egg mixture, stirring continuously so the egg does not cook and go lumpy. Preheat the oven to 180ºc or gas mark 5.

Pour the mixture into six ramekins or large cups and place in a deep tray. Pour hot water into the tray to just above half way up the ramekins. (This is known as a bain-marie).

Carefully place in the oven and cook for between 30-40 minutes, or until the creams have almost set – shake the tray gently and the creams should wobble a little like a jelly. Remove the creams from the bain-marie and chill.

Just before serving sprinkle over some demerara sugar and flash under the grill until the sugar starts to bubble and caramelise. Serve immediately.

CHAMPAGNE RHUBARB & GINGER ETON MESS

Serves four

INGREDIENTS

For the meringue:

50g egg white

100g caster sugar

Half teaspoon of ground ginger

For the rhubarb:

500g trimmed first season rhubarb

100g caster sugar

Vanilla extract

300ml double cream

30g caster sugar

1 vanilla pod

METHOD

To make the meringues: For best results pour boiling water over the bowl and the whisk (making sure you dry thoroughly before use) to get rid of any traces of grease which would prevent the egg whites from whipping. Whisk the egg whites until they form soft peaks and add 50g of the sugar. Whisk again until the meringue turns very glossy and will form firm peaks. Gently fold in the rest of the sugar together with the ginger. Put golf ball-sized spoonfuls of meringue onto a lined baking sheet and place in a preheated oven (120°c or gas mark 1). Leave for a couple of hours or until the meringues have dried out.

For the rhubarb: Thinly slice the rhubarb and place into a fairly deep baking tray. Sprinkle with the 100g sugar and a few drops of vanilla extract. Bake in a moderate oven until the rhubarb is soft and juicy. Leave to chill.

To serve: Whip the cream with the sugar, split the vanilla pod, scrape out the seeds and add to the cream. Whip to a soft peak. Roughly crush the meringues and gently fold into the cream. Layer the rhubarb with the cream/meringue mix in large wine glasses and serve immediately.

Note: The term 'champagne' rhubarb is used only for the very first pick of rhubarb when it is young, tender and has a lovely fresh pink colouring. Nothing to do with the bubbly stuff, although there is nothing to stop you serving a glass with this dessert because they complement each other. So here's a good excuse to open a bottle.

ECCLES CAKES

Serves eight

INGREDIENTS

1 sheet of ready made puff pastry

125g caster sugar

125g sultanas

125g currants

125g melted butter

2 teaspoons of ground nutmeg

2 teaspoons of ground cinnamon

2 slices of bread

50ml sherry

Granulated sugar for topping

METHOD

Blitz the bread into crumbs and mix with the currants, sultanas, sugar, butter and spices. Pour on the sherry and let soak in for a short while.

Roll out the pastry until quite thin and cut into eight squares. Divide the fruit mixture into eight and place in the centre of each square of pastry. Lightly dampen the edges with water. Bring the corners into the centre and nip together to form a seal. Turn the Eccles cake over and form a rough circle. Flatten out to about half an inch thick. Place onto a baking tray and brush the top of each cake with water and sprinkle generously with granulated sugar. Place into a preheated oven (200ºc or gas mark 8) and bake for 20-25 minutes until golden & crispy. Serve with vanilla ice cream and butterscotch sauce.

STEAMED SYRUP SPONGE

Serves four

INGREDIENTS

100g butter

100g caster sugar

2 eggs

150g self raising flour

6 tablespoons of golden syrup

Butter for greasing

METHOD

Lightly grease a two pint pudding bowl. Beat together 100g of butter with 100g of sugar until light and fluffy. Beat in the eggs one at a time, add a tablespoon of syrup and beat. Fold in the flour.

Pour the remainder of the syrup into the greased bowl and spoon the pudding mixture on top. Cover the basin with a piece of folded, greased foil and tie with some string or an elastic band over the lip of the bowl, to secure

Steam for about 1 hour 15 minutes. Pierce with a skewer. If the pudding is cooked the skewer should come out clean.

To turn out: Run a knife around the inner edge of the bowl, put a serving plate upside down over the bowl and turn bowl and plate over.

Serve with whipped or clotted cream.

JAM ROLY POLY

Serves four

INGREDIENTS

250g self raising flour

100g vegetarian suet

Half a teaspoon of salt

100-150ml milk

150g raspberry jam (approx)

METHOD

Sieve the flour into a bowl and add the salt and suet. Pour in the milk gradually to form a soft, but not sticky, dough. Roll the dough into a 25cm x 20cm rectangle and spread the jam over the dough leaving about 5cm around the edge. Roll up.

Wrap the roly poly loosely in grease proof paper and then loosely in foil, scrunch the foil at each end.

Steam the pudding for about 1 hour 15 minutes, not forgetting to top up the pan with more water if needed. Take the roly poly out of the greaseproof paper and foil, place on a baking tray and finish off in a preheated oven (200ºc, or gas mark 6) for 15-20 minutes. Check with a skewer, if it comes out clean the roly poly is ready.

Serve with lashings of fresh custard.

A FEW MORE RECIPES TO TRY...

FRESH MUSSELS WITH WHITE WINE, CREAM AND GARLIC

(MOULES MARINIERE) Serves four

2kg fresh mussels cleaned and beards removed
6 shallots finely sliced
4 cloves of garlic crushed
100g butter
400ml white wine
200ml double cream

This dish is easy, and only takes a few minutes to cook. First melt the butter in a deep pan and add the shallots and garlic, sauté until they start to turn golden. Pour in the washed mussels, shaking the pan to distribute the shallot and garlic, pour over the wine and place a tightly fitting lid on the pan. Cook for about 4-5 minutes shaking the pan every so often, remove the lid and check that the mussels have opened (if they have not replace the lid and cook for a further minute or so, any that don't open should be discarded). Share the mussels into your dishes and return the cooking liquor back to the heat and add the cream, bring to the boil and reduce a little. Pour over the mussels and serve immediately with lots of crusty French stick.

KING PRAWNS & MONKFISH WITH COCONUT, GINGER & SAMPHIRE

Serves four

12 king prawn tails
300g monkfish tail
1 thumb sized piece of fresh ginger grated
150g fresh samphire grass
200g tin coconut milk
2 spring onions finely chopped
1 red chilli very finely sliced
1 tablespoon of rice wine vinegar
Oil for cooking

Take the monkfish & cut it into 12 pieces, heat a little oil in a pan & gently lay in the monkfish & prawns, cook over a moderate heat to add a little colour. Add the spring onion, ginger, chilli & coconut milk, bring to the boil & add the samphire & rice wine vinegar, cook for a couple of minutes or until the sauce is syrupy & the fish is cooked.
To serve, share the prawns & monk between 4 plates & pour over the sauce & samphire. Serve with prawn crackers or rice
If you struggle to get fresh samphire you can buy pickled samphire in some supermarkets or deli's, just drain off the vinegar & don't add any rice wine vinegar & follow the recipe as normal.

PAN-SEARED MONKFISH WITH JERUSALEM ARTICHOKE AND LEMON OIL

Serves four

400g monkfish tail trimmed and skinned and cut
into 12 equal pieces
1kg Jerusalem artichokes
1 clove of garlic crushed
Milk for cooking the artichoke
Oil for pan searing the monkfish
150ml extra virgin olive oil
Juice and zest of 1 small lemon
Salt and pepper

Peel the artichokes and chop into equal size pieces
and place into a pan with the milk and garlic, bring
to the boil, cover with a lid and simmer until tender.
Strain off the milk and purée the artichoke with a

stick blender or a food processor, pass through a sieve
to remove any stringy pieces, season to taste. Set
aside and keep warm.

For the dressing, simply add the lemon juice and zest
to the extra virgin olive oil with a little salt and
pepper, shake well.

To cook the monkfish, heat a little oil in a pan, season
the monkfish and gently lay in the monkfish, pan fry
for about 2 minutes then turn over and pan fry for a
further 2 minutes.

To serve, place three spoonfuls of artichoke onto each
plate and sit the monkfish on top of the artichoke,
drizzle over the dressing and serve immediately.

SARDINES ON TOAST

Serves four

4 ciabatta rolls
24 fresh sardine fillets
6 shallots finely sliced
300ml passatta (sieved tomatoes)
50g butter
Pepper
Chopped parsley to finish
Oil for pan frying

Cut your Ciabatta in half and place under a
preheated grill and toast both sides, for best results
use 2 frying pans if you have them, if not do this
stage in two. Heat some oil in the pans and gently
lay in the sardines with the shallots, cook on one side
for about 2 minutes or until the outside starts to go a
little crispy, turn them over and cook for a further 2
minutes, then add the pasatta and butter. Reduce the
sauce a little and add the chopped parsley and pepper
if required. To serve, place 3 fillet of sardines on to
each piece of toasted Ciabatta and spoon a little sauce
over each. Serve immediately.

Sauces and Other Essentials

SWEET CHILLI SAUCE

600ml water

600g sugar

1 tablespoon of tomato ketchup

1 tablespoon of white wine vinegar

5 red chillies sliced very finely

Put the sugar, water, chillies and vinegar into a pan and bring to the boil. Reduce until the mixture is syrupy and coats the back of a spoon. Stir in the tomato ketchup and cool.

BALSAMIC DRESSING

100ml aged balsamic vinegar

100ml extra virgin olive oil

(oils made from kalamata olives are the best)

Salt and pepper

Mix the oil, vinegar, salt and pepper together by shaking vigorously until they emulsify. Season to taste.

MARIE ROSE SAUCE

350g mayonnaise

100g salad cream

150g tomato ketchup

1 teaspoon of lemon juice

1 teaspoon of Worcester sauce

Half a teaspoon of Tabasco sauce

Mix all the ingredients together.

Any unused sauce can be placed in an air tight jar and kept in the fridge for up to one week.

TARTARE SAUCE

500g mayonnaise

50g capers

150g gherkins

Juice of 1 lime

Half a teaspoon of Tabasco sauce

Half a teaspoon of Worcester sauce

1 sprig of parsley chopped

(to give about 1 heaped teaspoon)

Finely chop the capers, gherkins and parsley. Add to the mayonnaise with the lime juice, Tabasco and Worcester sauce and mix well.

HORSERADISH DRESSING

2 tablespoons of mayonnaise

1 tablespoon of horseradish sauce

1-2 tablespoons of water

Freshly milled black pepper

Mix the mayonnaise and horseradish together. Add enough water so the dressing is not too stiff. Check the seasoning and adjust to taste. This dressing will keep for up to five days in the fridge.

FISH STOCK

1kg fish bones

1 large onion

1 leek white part only

1 stick celery

Half a lemon

2-3 stalks of parsley

3-4 white peppercorns

1 bay leaf

30g butter

$2^1/_2$ ltrs water

Sweat (cook without colour) the vegetables and bones in the butter for about five minutes. Add the bay leaf, peppercorns, lemon, parsley and water. Bring to the boil, skimming if necessary. Reduce heat to a rapid simmer for 20 minutes.
Sieve the stock, pass through some muslin and chill.

FORTUNE'S WHITBY cured KIPPERS
ESTABLISHED 1872
Obtainable HERE ONLY
TEL 01947 601659

Fishermans 18 Cottage

THE MAGPIE CAFE

Captain's Quarters

Cooks Cottage
25

Whitby
St. Mary's Church
Lifeboat Museum
Sutcliffe Galle
Beach
Pannett Park
Indoor Pool

ART CENTRE

10 COBBLES COTTAGE
HOLIDAY LETTING
TEL. 01302 845037

BEACON FARM
Farm Shop

WHITBY FISH MARKET

WHITBY SEAFISH LTD
01947 841236

HENRIETTA STREET

NEWCASTLE UNITED

17 THE CRAGG

HARBOURS POTTERY

Currant Preserve
Extra Jam
Raspberry Preserve
Extra Jam

SPINDLETOP 115

DEFIANT
Whitby

Copious WY170

OPEN
FOR THE SALE O
KIPPER

DENNIS CROOKS
WHITBY (U.K.)
Tel: 01947 605677

KEEP CLOSED AT SEA

CROOKED COTTAGE

Magpie

THE MAGPIE CAF

THE OTHER MAGPIES

Anyone would think there was some sort of conspiracy over the name of the café. But The Magpie was named a good century before I first donned my black and white scarf and headed for St James' Park to cheer on…The Magpies.

So it's a coincidence, but as coincidences go, it's a gem – particularly as our head chef Paul Gildroy is almost as ardent a fan of the Toon as am I.

That dedication has been tested to the limit since you have to look back to 1969 to find the last major trophy in Newcastle United's cabinet. That was the year they won the Inter-Cities Fairs Cup.

So it's perhaps just as well that I'm not a glory hunter: It's not the pots and trophies, it's being part of a group and going to the games where you can abuse the ref – in a friendly way of course.

My allegiance was nurtured in childhood listening to my dad Eddie, a native of the Newcastle area, talking about his beloved Magpies. I followed them from about the age of five or six and when I was old enough to have a paper round I'd spend hours delivering the papers on a Sunday because I spent so much time reading reports of Toon matches in each of the papers.

It wasn't until I was 17 that I actually went to watch them play. It was against Manchester United and we lost. The trek from Whitby to Newcastle was long and arduous – a good two and a half hours away by train. It was expensive too, but worth every penny.

After that I tried to go to all the home games I could, but going to away matches was out of the question because of time and cost. These days I'm a season ticket holder and I go to as many games as the demands of the café allow.

I've always thought that we're like a big family at the Magpie and that's the case whether we're talking about food or football. Guess which team Paul's wife Lindsay is potty about?

The passion extends to their toddler daughter Maya, who has her own seat and goes to matches where she claps and cheers with an enthusiasm matched only by her mum and dad.

Paul always tells me the match is the ideal antidote to the stress of the kitchen at full throttle – he gets lost in the excitement of it all. All emotions, passion, sorrows are taken out on the ref.

For entertainment closer to home, let's not forget Whitby Town, which we help and support almost as fervently as Newcastle. Here's hoping they both do well.

AN ARTISTIC
POINT OF VIEW

I came to Whitby as a stranger in the winter days of 2008/2009. I left it two weeks later feeling I had found a second home. I'd heard numerous stories before this, my first ever visit. Everyone I met seemed to have some connection, some affinity, some story about the place. In every case, the Magpie Café was mentioned in the same breath.

What particularly struck me was the sense of deep community that people shared – everywhere I went, everyone I photographed seemed to have grown up in Whitby passing on their trade to their children, living with good friendships that went back for years. The newcomer is quickly made welcome, and in true Yorkshire fashion, reserve is cast aside. There were conversations with the fisherman on the street who stopped me and talked photography, staff and diners at the Magpie, locals who were proud of their town.

Whitby is a well-documented subject for photographers, and of course is synonymous with one of the greatest, Frank Meadow Sutcliffe, whose work appears elsewhere in this book. I wanted to capture Whitby in a slightly different way; images that would tell the story of the town, from the details of the lobster pots to the landscapes of the Abbey and the harbour. I was there in November and January, so the sun was low and watery and the dusk fell early in the day, creating beautiful skies.

And of course, there was the privilege of working with two professionals in the shape of Ian and Paul, recreating the dishes that have made the Magpie Café world famous.

I wanted those who love the landscapes and monuments of Whitby to be drawn again to see their home town in all its beauty and character. Talking this over with Ian was a pleasure, his keen interest in photography gave me a few insights into some local scenic secrets. I also wanted to entice those who, like me, had never been to Whitby before, to make the journey. You will not be disappointed.

Jodi Hinds
www.jodihinds.com

MISSED OUT ON THE FIRST MAGPIE CAFÉ COOK BOOK?

With more than 15,000 copies sold, the Magpie Café Cook book was a huge hit with lovers of good seafood and fish dishes. Such was the demand that copies are now hard to come by.

But if you've enjoyed this book and would like to see more, the original book is now available in a digital edition for only £5. So just follow the link at www.magpiecafe.co.uk for more of the recipes that made the Magpie famous.